W9-DIA-697

Light Upon Light

Light Upon Light

Inspirations from RUMI

ANDREW HARVEY

Photographs by
Eryk Hanut

JEREMY P. TARCHER/PENGUIN
a member of
Penguin Group (USA) Inc.

Prints of the photographs by Eryk Hanut reproduced in this book are available for purchase. For more information, please contact:

Balthazar Productions
3739 Balboa Street, 182
San Francisco, California 94121
FAX: (415) 386-9078

For information on limited edition and gelatin silver prints,
please contact:

Kristina Grace
Spirit in Form Gallery
285 Missouri Street
San Francisco, California 94107
Tel: (415) 626-4132

Most Tarcher/Penguin books are available at special quantity discounts for bulk purchases for sales promotions, premiums, fund-raising, and educational needs. Special books or book excerpts also can be created to fit specific needs. For details, write Penguin Group (USA) Inc., Special Markets, 375 Hudson Street, New York, NY 10014.

Jeremy P. Tarcher/Penguin
a member of
Penguin Group (USA) Inc.
375 Hudson Street
New York, NY 10014
www.penguin.com

First published in 1996 by North Atlantic Books, Berkeley, California

First Jeremy P. Tarcher/Penguin Edition 2004

Copyright © 1996 by Andrew Harvey
All rights reserved. This book, or parts thereof, may not
be reproduced in any form without permission.
Published simultaneously in Canada

Light Upon Light: Inspirations from Rumi is sponsored by the Society for the Study of Native Arts and Sciences, a nonprofit educational corporation whose goals are to develop an educational and crosscultural perspective linking various scientific, social, and artistic fields; to nurture a holistic view of the arts, sciences, humanities, and healing: and to publish and distribute literature on the relationship of mind, body, and nature.

An application to register this book for cataloguing
has been submitted to the Library of Congress.
ISBN 1-58542-298-3 (paperback edition)

Printed in the United States of America
1 3 5 7 9 10 8 6 4 2

Book design by Paula Morrison

For Sandra Mosbacher-Smith,
In eternal gratitude and love.

Andrew Harvey
Eryk Hanut

For Rumi

O Prince of Beauty! Make your subjects radiant!
Give life to our fistfuls of nothing!
The army of Agony blackens the horizon—
Make triumph the Joy of the Holder of the Standard!

—from the *Diwan*

Contents

Introduction

When the great Sufi mystic and poet Jalal-ud-Din Rumi died at sunset in Konya, southern Turkey, on December 17, 1273, he had lived for almost half his sixty-six years in the Sun of the Awakened Heart. With the light of its splendor as his constant inspiration, Rumi composed 3,500 odes, 2,000 quatrains, and a vast spiritual epic called the *Mathnawi*, and founded the Mevlevi Order that, under his son Sultan Walad and his successors, was to spread his vision throughout the Islamic world, from the most remote villages of Turkey and Iran to Jakarta, from Tangiers to Sarajevo. Now, over 700 years later, through the pioneering (and superb) translations of Coleman Barks, Robert Bly, Jonathan Star, and others, Rumi is almost as well known and revered in the West as he has long been in the East.

Not long before his death, Rumi wrote of his passion for his Beloved, Shams-I-Tabriz, and its significance:

> *Those tender words we said to one another*
> *Are stored in the secret heart of heaven.*
> *One day, like the rain, they will fall and spread*
> *And their mystery will grow green over the world.*

The time has come for this greening of the world's heart and mind by the mystery of Rumi's love for his Beloved. Increasingly, Rumi is being recognized as the unique spiritual genius he is, as someone who fused at the highest level and with the greatest possible intensity the intellect of a Plato, the vision, passion, and soul-force of a Christ or Buddha, and the extraordinary literary gifts of a Shakespeare. Rumi is, I believe, not only the world's greatest mystic poet but also an essential guide to the new planetary spiritual renaissance that is slowly emerging from the ruins of our civilization. He speak to us from the depths of our own sacred identity, and what he says has the electric eloquence of our own innermost truth. No other poet or teacher or philosopher of whom I know has Rumi's almost frightening intimacy of address, and no one I am aware of in any civilization has conveyed the terror, rapture, and wonder of awakening to Divine Love with such fearless and gorgeous courage, such humility, and such unflinching clarity.

Our shared planetary future depends on our taking—alone and together, and soon—the journey into Love. There is no wiser, more astute, or more inspiring guide to this journey than Rumi. *Light Upon Light* is a distillation of twenty years' devotion and love for Rumi's work in all its forms—poems, table-talk, letters—into an arrangement that can convey the range of his wisdom as passionately and comprehensively as possible. I have selected those passages and poems which have most shaken and helped me in my own search, and organized them into a five-part mystical symphony. The texts are presented in a complex musical order and unfolding that mirrors the order and unfolding of the mystical journey into Love itself. I hope to communicate the authentic rhythms of awakening, with its alternating, mutually illuminating periods of expansion and contraction, passion and discipline, ecstasy and necessary—and repeated—ordeal.

In this selection, I have especially emphasized an aspect of Rumi's work which I believe is crucial to us now—its fierce and humble rigor. Rumi is never sentimental; he suffered hugely for his illumination and knew that the mystery of accepting grief and death had to be learned in the furnace of a transformation that burns away all illusion. There is a seared and sometimes ferocious honesty about his testimony to the mystical life that we all need to listen to and tune ourselves by. Especially in a time and world like ours, where fantasy, frivolity, exaggeration, and imprecision are rampant, and the difficulties of real spiritual growth are too often shirked or scanted.

I have worked from literal and scholarly versions of the texts, along with more literary translations of all kinds in several languages. My primary sources include the work of A. J. Arberry, E. H. Whinfield, R. A. Nicholson, and W. C. Chittick, and the marvelous French translations of Eva de Vitray-Meyerovitch. On rare occasions I have cut or added where I think Rumi's intention demands it. The longer poems come from the *Diwan of Shams-I-Tabriz* or the *Mathnawi,* the great majority of the longer prose passages from the *Discourses,* the quatrains from the *Rubaiyat,* and a few short passages from Rumi's letters. The brief quotations that pepper the text are nearly always from the *Odes* or the *Discourses.*

Ideally, I would like *Light Upon Light* to be read alongside my earlier work *The Way of Passion: A Celebration of Rumi,* in which I try to give my vision of how Rumi can be approached most richly and deeply. Friends who have read *Light Upon Light* in manuscript tell me the best way of entering it is to read it all the way through several times, slowly and intensely, in order to experience—and inwardly recreate—its musical progression, and then to concentrate on clusters of different poems and passages. In this way, reading the book can become a way of allowing Rumi's vision to saturate slowly one's heart and mind.

The world is in terrible danger. We have very little time left in which to make desperately needed changes in every arena of life. We need the truth and empowerment of authentic mystical understanding and love now more than at any other moment of our history. May the Light of the Heart be revealed in and to all of us, and may we all, united in and by Divine Love, transform together the conditions of life on earth.

Andrew Harvey
January 1996

*I dedicate this Introduction to Carol Ricotta, in gratitude
for the example of her courage and unwavering love of justice.*

FIRST MOVEMENT

The Call

If You Are Seeking

 If you are seeking, seek us with joy
For we live in the kingdom of joy.
Do not give your heart to anything else
But to the love of those who are clear joy,
Do not stray into the neighborhood of despair.
For there are hopes: they are real, they exist—
Do not go in the direction of darkness—
I tell you: suns exist.

There doesn't exist a being Your grace cannot transfigure,
And the Lover You choose lives in joy forever.
What atom could Your Grace even for a moment come near
Without making it more magnificent than a thousand suns?

All theologies are straws His Sun burns to dust;
Knowing takes you to the Threshold, but not through the Door.
Nothing can teach you if you don't unlearn everything
How learned I was, before Revelation made me dumb.

The Real Sun

The sun you see in the sky is imitative and metaphorical; there is a far more real sun that is manifesting everything. Everything is one of its rays, everything is born from this sun and dies back into it. It is this sun you should yearn for, so that you can come to see something more than just sense-objects, and so your knowledge can go on and on growing.

There is another sun, apart from the sun of physical form, a sun through which inner truths and realities are unveiled. Any partial knowledge that enthralls you is a branch of that great knowledge and a ray of it. And this ray is summoning you to that great knowledge and that Sun of Origin.

"There are those who are called from afar."

You draw that knowledge towards yourself. This knowledge says: "I cannot be contained here in this world, and you are taking your time arriving in my world. It is impossible for me to be contained in your world, and you will find it difficult to arrive in mine." Do not despair. Bringing about the impossible is impossible; succeeding in the difficult is not. So, although it is difficult, strive to attain the great knowledge, and never expect it to be contained here in any way, for that is impossible.

What is the goal of all of this? Imagine a tree whose roots are fixed firmly in the garden of Spirit. Its branches and boughs have become suspended elsewhere, and its fruits have been scattered. What is essential is that these fruits should be brought back to the garden, where the roots of the tree are. The tree might outwardly sing God's praises and do all sorts of devotional exercises, but if its roots are really in this world, then its fruit will be brought back into this world, too. If both roots and fruit are in that world and that garden, then there is Light upon Light.

Oh Life of the Soul! Since you have a house
In every atom of this world,
Why doesn't the dust of the road sing?
Why are stones shut down?
Why does poison taste terrible?
Why do thorns pierce?
Why does anger flame into violence?
Why are nights black?
One day in the garden of Your Face
I couldn't keep from being amazed
At how, during Your Reign,
A thorn could still be a thorn.
"Has He," I thought, "out of self-jealousy,
Masked His own face?
Does He sustain this 'otherness'
So others cannot glimpse Him at all?
Or is it that the world's eye
Is so cancered-over, so darkened,
It can see nothing, nothing at all,
Of the tenderness of that radiant Face?"

You haven't dared yet lose faith—so how can faith
    grow in you?
You haven't dared yet risk your heart—so what can
    you see of reality?
You're obsessed—still!—with the carnal screams
    of your life.
How do you hope to step into the Mystery of the King?

You are a sea of gnosis hidden in a drop of dew,
You are a whole universe hidden in a sack of blood.
What are all this world's pleasures and joys
That you keep grasping at them to make you alive?
Does the sun borrow light from a mote of dust?
Does Venus look for wine from a cracked jug?

There is no angel so sublime, He whispered,
Who can be granted for one moment
What is granted you forever.
And I hung my head, astounded.

The Emperor and the Hawk

When a poacher lays a trap and snares little birds in it to eat and sell—that you can convincingly call cunning. But if an emperor lays a trap to catch an ignorant, worthless hawk, which has no awareness of its intrinsic nature, in order to teach it himself, on his own wrist, so that it can become noble, aware, and bright-eyed with pure, fearless knowledge—that you cannot call cunning. It may *seem* like cunning, but in fact it is the height of Truth, Justice, and Magnanimity; it is an act that deserves to be called "Resurrection" because it does nothing less than bring the dead to life, and can be called "Alchemy" because it transforms an ordinary stone into the richest of rubies. If a hawk knew why the emperor wanted to catch it, there wouldn't be any need for bait and a trap; with a wild glad heart it would look for the trap itself and fly through lightning and thunder to the wrist of the king.

Leap Free of the Cage

How could the soul not take flight
When from the glorious Presence
A soft call flows sweet as honey,
And whispers, "Rise up now, come away."
How could the fish not jump
Immediately from dry land into water,
When the sound of water from the ocean
Of fresh waves springs to his ear?
How could the hawk not fly away,
Back, back, to the wrist of the king
As soon as he hears the drum
The king's baton hits again and again,
Drumming out the signal of return?
How could the Sufi not start to dance,
Turning on himself, like the atom in the sun of eternity,
So he can leap free of this dying world?
Fly away, fly away, bird, to your native home.
You have leaped free of the cage,
Your wings are flung back in the wind of God.
Leave behind the stagnant and marshy waters,
Hurry, hurry, hurry, O bird, to the source of life!

Destroy Yourself

Destroy your own house, destroy it now!
Don't wait one more minute! Pull the whole house down!
A treasure greater than Pharaoh's is hidden under it.
Go and build with that a million houses!
In the end, whether you like it or not,
Your house will be pulled down and destroyed,
And the treasure under it revealed.
But then it will not belong to you—
For you can only own the treasure
If you destroy your house yourself.
How can you get the pay if you haven't done the work?
Do you imagine the Koran is speaking lightly when it says,
"Human beings don't get anything they haven't worked for"?

Time's tailor has never made a robe for anyone
Without then slashing it to pieces.
See how the million fools of this world
Pay Satan heaps of gold for pain!
Don't stretch out your legs on this earth-carpet,
It is a borrowed bed; fear that day
His messengers come to roll it up forever....
How can you go on gazing at the body's dust?
Search out the Horseman of the Soul!
Train your vision with passion and longing,
And see the Horseman at the heart of this dust-storm!

We are darkness and God is Light; this house
Receives all splendor from the Sun.
Here, the Light is mingled with shadow.
Do you want your light totally pure?
Leave the house and climb onto the roof.

You have seen the shapes the dust makes—
Now, see the Wind.
You have seen the foam, churning—
Now, see the Ocean of Flaming Power!

Terrible destruction dances and the world's days darken.
If you want Supreme Reality, hide from fame.
You're looking for the Pearl? Plunge, now, to the sea's bottom.
What's on the shore is only foam.

All of created existence is drunk on the Heart
The entire cosmos is a toy in Its hands.
All the nine levels of the spheres of Heaven
Are only two short steps for the Heart.

Speculation and grief find no life or support
Here where wine dances and soul-music plays.
O my heart-friends, taste deep of Eternal Joy!
Like flowers and grasses, bow your lips to the stream.

Same Moon

Generations have passed and this is a new generation. The moon is always the same, only the water changes. Justice remains the same justice, learning the same learning, as people and nations change.

Generations have passed; the true meanings stay constant and are eternal. The water in the stream may have changed a million times— the reflection of the moon and stars stays the same.

Different Paths, One Goal

There are a myriad different ways to search, but the object of the search is always the same. Don't you see that the roads to Mecca are all different? One comes from Byzantium, another from Syria, still others wind through land or across the sea. The roads are different; the goal is one.

When people reach the goal, all quarrels or disputes that flared along the road are resolved. Those who yelled at each other along the road, "You are wrong!" or "You are a blasphemer!" forget all possible differences when they reach the goal. There all hearts sing in unison.

One, One, One

The lamps are different,
But the Light is the same.
So many garish lamps in the dying brain's lamp-shop,
Forget about them.
Concentrate on the essence, concentrate on the Light.
In lucid bliss, calmly smoking off its own holy fire,
The Light streams towards you from all things,
All people, all possible permutations of good, evil,
    thought, passion.
The lamps are different,
But the Light is the same.
One matter, one energy, one Light, one Light-mind,
Endlessly emanating all things.
One turning and burning diamond,
One, one, one.
Ground yourself, strip yourself down,
To blind loving silence.
Stay there, until you see
You are gazing at the Light
With its own ageless eyes.

The Real King

There was a dervish once who entered the presence of a king. The king started to pay him tribute and said, "O ascetic."

The dervish quickly interrupted, "*You* are the ascetic."

"Me?" the king gasped, astonished, "How am I an ascetic, seeing that the whole earth is mine?"

The dervish smiled, "You see things the opposite of how they really are. This world and the next one, and everything in both, belongs to me. I have taken into my possession all the worlds. What you have become satisfied with is a handful of dust and rags."

> My heart, that dervish vagabond,
> Poured me the wine of oblivion.
> I staggered toward the House of Wine
> Dancing, dancing, dragging this old cloak.

Flash by Flash

What is the point of reaching the sea and being satisfied with a tiny jug of water? There are pearls in the sea, and from the sea heaps of ravishing, strange, and precious things can be won. And you are satisfied with just taking some water? You call yourself intelligent? Consider this world as it really is—just a bubble of foam of that great sea, and think: where is the pearl itself? This world is foam flecked with swirling flotsam; because the waves turn and churn continually, the foam comes to take on shapes of different kinds of beauty. This beauty is borrowed; its real essence is elsewhere. It is counterfeit coin, valueless and worthless, made by divine magic to appear wonderful.

Human beings are the astrolabe of God, but a real astronomer is required to know how to use the astrolabe. What would a grocer do with an astrolabe, and what happiness could he derive from it? How could he utilize so subtle a thing and come to know through it the secrets of the movements of the heavens, of the planets and their influences, powers, combinations, and transits? In the hands of a real astronomer, the astrolabe reveals marvel after marvel, for he who knows himself knows his Lord.

A copper astrolabe, then, is a mirror of the heavens; a human being is the astrolabe of God. When God graces a human being gnosis of Him, and brings that human being to know Him and be intimate with Him, then through the astrolabe of his own being he perceives, moment by moment, flash by flash, the flaming-out of God and His Infinite Beauty, and that beauty is never absent from his mirror.

How can you ever hope to know the Beloved
Without becoming in every cell the Lover?
And when you are the Lover at last, you don't care.
Whatever you know, or don't—only Love is real.

Last night a friend asked me, "Where is your homeland?"
I said nothing, for what could I say?
My homeland is not Egypt or Syria or Iraq.
My homeland's a place that has never had a name.

Root my being in certainty
So I witness You without fear.
Even as the waves of blood crash over me
And the worlds char in fire.

The One Thing You Must Never Forget

There is one thing in the world which you must never forget. If you were to forget everything else and remembered this, then you would have nothing at all to worry about; but if you were to remember everything else and then forget this, you would have done nothing with your life.

It is as if a king sent you to a country to carry out a particular mission. You go to that country, you do a hundred different things; but if you do not perform the mission assigned to you, it is as if you have done nothing. All human beings have come into the world for a particular mission, and that mission is our singular purpose. If we do not enact it, we have done nothing.

In the Koran, God says: "We offered the Trust to the heavens, the earth, and the mountains. They refused it, and were afraid; and man carried it. In all truth, man is full of sin and folly."

"We offered the Trust to the heavens, but they could not accept it." Think for a moment how many things are done by the heavens, at which human reason reels in amazement. The heavens transform ordinary stones into rubies; the heavens make mountains into mines of gold and silver; the heavens make herbs and grasses grow and dance into life, turning the earth into a Garden of Eden. Think of the earth, too, how it receives seed and breaks into blossom and fruit; how it covers up all wounds and imperfections; how it accepts and unveils incessantly a hundred thousand miracles that no tongue could ever fully enumerate. All these things the heavens and the earth perform, yet the one thing God speaks of is not performed by them. That supreme mission is humankind's.

God says in the Koran, "And we honored the Children of Adam." God did not say, "And we honored heaven and earth." That mission that the heavens and earth cannot enact is meant to be enacted by humankind. And when a person carries out that mission, "sin" and "folly"—the sin and folly instinctual to his nature—run away from him.

Now, if you were to say, "Look, even if I have not performed this mission I have, after all, performed a hundred others," that would mean nothing. You were not created for those other missions. It is as if you were to buy a sword of priceless Indian steel such as one usually finds only in the treasuries of emperors, and were to turn it into a butcher's knife for cutting up rotten meat, saying, "Look, I'm not letting this sword stay unused, I am putting it to a thousand highly useful purposes." Or it is as though you were to take a golden bowl and cook turnips in it, while for just one grain of that gold you could purchase hundreds of pots.

Or it is as though you were to take a dagger of the most finely-wrought and tempered steel and use it as a nail to hang a broken pitcher on, saying, "I'm making excellent use of my dagger. I'm hanging a broken pitcher on it, after all. It is not standing useless." How absurd and how sad that would be! When you can hang a picture on a nail that costs only a few cents, what sense does it make to use a dagger worth a fortune?

God the Omnipotent, the Glorious, has set a very high price on each one of you, for in His Book He says, "God has purchased their selves and possessions from the believers, and given in their stead the gift of Paradise."

The poet says:

> You are more valuable than both heaven and earth.
> What else can I say? You don't know your own worth.
> Do not sell yourself at a ridiculous price,
> You who are so valuable in God's eyes.

God is always saying to you, "Look, I have purchased you— each moment of your life, each breath, all of your possessions and lives. And if you spend all of them on me, if you offer them to me, I will give you in exchange—Paradise. Realize how infinitely I value you."

How long will you move backward? Come forward; do not stray in unbelief, come dancing to Divine Knowledge. Look, the elixir is hidden in the poison, come to the poison and come, return to the root of the root of your own self.

You think you are earthly beings, but you have been kneaded from the Light of Certainty. You are the guardians of God's Light, so come, return to the root of the root of your own self.

Once you have tied yourself to selflessness, you will be delivered from selfhood and released from the teeth of a hundred snares. So come, return to the root of the root of your own self.

You were born vice-regent of the children of God, but you have lowered your eyes to this sad world; how can you be happy with these scraps? Come, return to the root of the root of your own self.

You are the talisman protecting the world's treasure; within yourself you are the Mine. Open your hidden eyes and come, return to the root of your own self.

You were born of the rays of God's majesty and have won the grace of your auspicious star; how long will you suffer at the hands of things that do not exist? Come, return to the root of the root of your own self.

Mary and Gabriel

When Mary saw Gabriel, she became terrified and cried out
(She was alone, and half-clothed, and feared the worst)—
"I take refuge in Divine Protection!"
Mary grew tormented, like a fish on dry land.
Then Gabriel, Icon of Divine Generosity, said to her:
"I am the faithful messenger of God! Don't run away!"
(And while Gabriel was speaking to her, a ray
Of pure light broke from his lips and soared to Arcturus.)
"You are running away from me," he went on, "to the invisible
    world;
I am King there, and the Bearer of the Standard.
You take refuge from me in God, yet in eternity I am
The image of He who is the only refuge.
I am that refuge that was often your deliverance.
You look for refuge against me; I am myself that refuge."

SECOND MOVEMENT

The Possibility

Another World Altogether

God has created all causes, in such a way that to a drop of sperm that did not possess either hearing, or intelligence, or spirit, or sight, or grief, or joy, or superiority, or inferiority, He has given a shelter in the womb. There, He transformed water into blood and coagulated and modeled that blood into skin; and there, where there were no hands or limbs of any kind before He created the windows of the mouth, eyes, and ears, fashioned the tongue and throat, and the chest's cave in which he placed a heart that is, all at once, a drop and a world, pearl and ocean, slave and king. What intelligence exists that could understand how He could lead us from such a miserable place and state of ignorance to where we are now?

God has said, "Have you seen or heard from where I have taken you and will take you? I tell you that I will not leave you even where you are now; I will lead you beyond this heaven and this earth, into a purer heaven and earth that you cannot imagine, whose nature is to expand the soul in joy. In the heart of this new heaven what is young and fresh never withers, what is new never loses its luster, nothing grows corrupted or falls into ruin, nothing dies, no one who has once awoken ever sleeps again, because sleep is made for rest and the scattering of grief, and here there is no exhaustion or grief.

And if you do not believe what I am saying, just think for a moment: how could that drop of sperm have believed you if you had told it that God had created another world outside its world of darkness, a world where there is a sky, a sun, moonlight, provinces, towns, villages, gardens; where there exist created beings—kings and millionaires, people in fine health, sick people, the blind?"

No intelligence would believe such a far-fetched story—and yet there exists, outside these shadows and this food of blood, another world altogether and quite another food. And although the drop of sperm ignored and denied such a possibility, yet it could not avoid arriving at it, because it was forced outside.

One day, you will find yourself outside this world which is like a womb. You will leave this earth to enter, while you are still in the body, a vast expanse, and you *will* know that the words "God's earth is vast" describe this region from which the saints have come.

The Real Miracles

It isn't so amazing or miraculous for someone to be able to go from here to Mecca in an afternoon or a moment. The wind, after all, performs such a miracle: in an afternoon, or a moment, it can go wherever it wants.

The real miracle is that God should take you from a low and miserable stage to the highest honor, that you should come from there to here, from ignorance to reason, from selfishness to adoration, from the unliving to life. At first you were earth, then mineral, and then His power brought you into the vegetable world; then you traveled from there to the world of sperm and womb, and from there to the animal world, and from the animal world into the human one. The real miracles are those that occur on the journey in God to God. All the experiences and openings you had on the way—could you have even begun to imagine them before they happened? Did you have any idea what roads you would take before you took them? Yet you have definitely arrived here.

In exactly the same way, and with exactly the same mercy and mystery and strange providence, you will be brought to thousands of other worlds.

Have faith, always, and if you are told stories of such worlds by people you trust—believe them.

Hollow Drum

 This world is like a drum; people marvel at its sound and crowd around. In fact, the drum is hollow, has no skin, and no real interest. Happy is the man who has found the Perfume-Maker's House and whose heart has grown cold to the rat-a-tat of the drum of this world.

From one horizon to another, this world breeds only grief.
Frivolous fool! Don't go looking for suffering—
Even if you could make the sun and moon a crown for your head,
When you die, you'll still prop your head on a brick.

Each Breath a Treasure

"Be strenuous now, so when death arrives
It finds the perfume of your soul near the Beloved."

In the Koran, God says: "He who has done an atom of good will see it." This world is the seed-time of the Beyond. If you are lazy at seed-time, you weep at harvest, when all tears are futile.

It is today, now, that we must use and profit from each breath, for each of our breaths is a treasure, the philosopher's stone. Spend each breath on the Path to God and never grow desperate.

Love for the Creator is latent in all human beings and in everything in the world, in fact in all things that have being. How could anyone not love the One who gave him or her being? Love is latent in every human being, but obstructions veil that love; when those obstructions are taken away, love flashes out and becomes real.

Why am I only speaking of things that have being? Non-being too is in tumult, passionate to be given being by Him. Imagine four people before a king. Each one feels shy of the others, because his or her expectation is at odds to what the others want. So they all feel shy of each other, for each wants to be the first to be brought into being, and each cries out secretly: "Make me be!" If this is the situation with non-beings, imagine what the things that do have being are feeling. As the Koran says, "There is nothing that does not proclaim His praise."

This is not to be wondered at; what is to be wondered at is that there is no *no-thing* that does not proclaim his praise.

Both unbelief and faith are seeking you.

And both proclaim your undivided Oneness.

There are two kinds of intellect; the first is acquired—
Thanks to it, you learn like a schoolboy
Books, teachers, reflection, concepts, all kinds of
    sciences . . .
You learn and your intellect grows superior.
But conserving this knowledge is always a burden.
The other intellect is God's pure gift;
Its heart is in the breast of the soul.
When the water of divine gnosis jets from the heart
It never becomes stagnant or old or dirty.
And if it can't flow outside, what does that matter?
It keeps foaming up from within the heart.

There's an intellect like the sun's blazing disc—
And one inferior to Venus or a shooting star.
There's an intellect like a flickering lamp,
And one like a brilliant star of fire,
That when all clouds are pulled back from Its Face
Births eyes that contemplate the Light of God.

Have the Courage to Say "God"

Human beings are in love with what they have never seen or heard or understood; day and night, they hunger for it, run after it. I myself am the slave of the One I cannot see; I myself am one who is exhausted from always running from what I have seen and understood. Philosophers deny that God can be seen; if He could be seen, they point out, then eyes could also weary of Him and that cannot be possible. Sunni theologians say that He can only really be seen in the moment when He appears one-colored, since in every other moment He is appearing in a thousand colors.

What I know, however, is this: if God revealed himself a hundred thousand times, not one of them would resemble another. In God, everything is always new-minted, fresh-born. You are actually seeing God this moment; every moment you are seeing God's thousand colors displayed in His works and acts. Not one of God's acts resembles any other. Joy is one of His epiphanies, so is grieving, so is fear, so is hope. Just as the acts of God and the epiphany of His acts and works are infinitely varied, so the epiphany of His Essences is also infinitely varied.

I remember this verse from the Koran, "It is We who have sent down the Remembrance and it is we who stand guard over it."

For me, this verse means: "We have placed in your core a seeking and a longing. We stand guard over them, so they are not wasted but are brought to fruition."

Have the courage to say "God" once, and stand firm under all the catastrophes that then rain down upon you. A man came to Mohammed and said, "I sincerely love you." The Prophet said, "Take care what you say." The man repeated, "I sincerely and deeply love you." Again the Prophet said, "Take care what you say." The man repeated, "I sincerely love you." "Good," said the Prophet, "now stand firm while I kill you with my own hands."

Another man said to Mohammed, "I do not want your religion. Take it back. Ever since I entered it I have not had a single day of peace. I've lost my money, my wife, my child, all the respect I had, all the strength, all the passion." The Prophet replied, "Wherever our religion has gone it does not return without uprooting a person utterly and sweeping clean his house."

As the Koran says, "No one but the purified shall touch it." God is the final Beloved. As long as there remains in you a single hair of self-love, God will not and cannot show the glory of His face to you; you will not be worthy of union with Him and He will not unveil Himself to you. Become dead to yourself and the world, become your own shrewdest and most implacable enemy, so then, at last, He may show you His face.

To return to the man who was complaining of the path, and the suffering it brought, the Prophet said to him, "The grieving you are going through is a purging of the illusions that have enslaved you and made you a prisoner of your false self. Imagine you had eaten something poisonous—wouldn't a doctor give you something to purge it, and wouldn't he say to you, 'Eat nothing until your stomach has discharged its poison'? When all the poison has left, then you can eat." So be patient, and let yourself grieve: grieving is a purgation. After it, great joy will visit you, a joy that has no pain, that is a thornless rose, a wine that leaves no headache.

You are looking for peace in a world that cannot give it to you. Whatever comfort or consolation any of us finds in this world passes like a lightning flash. And there are so many kinds of lightning, too—lightning full of snow, full of hail, full of rain; lightning full of death and torment. Think of a man setting out for Antalya: he heads in the direction of Caesarea, hoping to reach Antalya, and travels on and on blindly, ignorant of the fact that he can never reach his destination. The man who heads out on the Antalya road, however weak he is, or lame, will reach his goal since it is at the end of the road.

No important worldly task can be accomplished without pain,

so how could the Supreme Task not be hard to bring to completion? You have to suffer, one way or the other. There is no way out. At least devote your suffering to finding that Door of Adoration, which is the only way out. You are going to die anyway; why not die, while you are alive, into the Life that will never die, into the Love that is Eternal Life?

What is the essential spirit of all sciences?
To know who you will be on the Day of Resurrection!

Whip up the waves of non-being and wash me away!
How long will I walk up and down the shore in fear?

If one drop of Divine Drunkenness fell
On the intellects of everyone in the world,
The world and its beings, free will, and obedience—
All, all, would vanish in a moment.

God has a hidden wine, my friend, and one
Of its drops became you and the world.
The next time He lets one drop of this wine fall,
You'll be sprung free of this world, the next, yourself.

Mid-Way

There are three kinds of creature. First—angels. Angels are pure intelligence. Their nature and their nourishment are worship, service, and perpetual remembrance of God. They eat and live by these exactly like fish live in and by water. Angels are under no burden of obligation. They have no desire, so they have no need to struggle against it. And while they obey God's will, they are not considered to be "obedient"; obedience is their essence.

Then there are animals. They are pure desire, desire in its naked state, unmediated by anything we know as moral intelligence.

Now comes poor, baffled, humankind—that strange hybrid of intelligence and desire. Man is half-beast, half-angel. The fish in man attracts him toward the shining water; the serpent in him drags him toward the earth. No wonder he is always in turmoil, always in battle, with himself and others. "He whose intelligence conquers his desires is higher than the angels; he whose desire overwhelms his intelligence sinks lower than any animal."

The angel is always saved by knowledge; the animal by its un-adorned ignorance. Man is between them, struggling, suffering, aspiring, failing, confused, desperate, ambiguous. What a predicament!

There are some human beings who follow their innate God-given intelligence so doggedly that they become entirely angels, entirely Pure Light. These are the prophets and saints and holy ones, the Friends and true Lovers. They have been saved from both fear and hope. As the Koran says, "No fear shall walk with them, nor will they grieve."

Lightning Flash

Your task? To work with all the passion of your being to acquire an inner light, so you escape and are safe from the fires of madness, illusion, and confusion that are, and always will be, the world.

When you have acquired this light, then every kind of power, all rank, status, and every conceivable reward the world could offer you will pass like a flash of lightning when they shine on your heart, in the same way as the fear of God and longing for the real world of holiness pass like a lightning flash when they shine on the hearts of the worldly.

If you are one of the People of God, you will be preoccupied with and absorbed by nothing but God. All worldly desires will be to you like the lusts of a man who cannot get an erection; they will not be able to take real root and will shrivel.

Go forward, knowing the Path will vanish under you
Open your arms, knowing they will burn away
Give everything you are, knowing it is nothing
Bathe always in His river, even when it's blood.

If anyone had once, even once, glimpsed Your Face of
    Lightning,
They'd spend every second stammering Your Praise.
Each moment, like the angels, they'd offer their heart to
    Your Fire,
Each moment, like the angels, they'd be reborn in You.

The sail of the ship of man's being is belief.
When there is a sail, the wind can carry him
To place after place of power and wonder.
No sail, all words are wind.

The Use of Words

You may ask: what then is the use of words? They set you searching and excite you to search. The goal of searching can never be attained through words. If that were the case, there would be no need of so much striving and passion, prayer and longing, and constant, consistent self-annihilating before the Glory of the Face. Think of words like something moving mysteriously in the distance: you run after it, hoping to see it more clearly. You do not in any way understand it through its movement.

Human speech can excite you to seek the meaning, but it is not the meaning itself, and you do not see what is being spoken of immediately and in reality. If what all men secretly long and hunger for—the essence of essences and the light of splendor—could be knowable simply by words, you would never need to die to your false self and to suffer such distress in looking for what you do not yet know you secretly are and possess. How much you have to endure for yourself not to remain, so that you come to know that which remains forever!

The Absolute Being creates out of non-existence; what other
    workshop
But non-existence could the Creator of Existence have?
Do you write over what is already written?
Do you plant a sapling where there's one growing already?
No! So look for a piece of paper no one has written on;
Search for a place where nothing has ever been sown.
Be a place unsown, a white paper no writing has stained,
So the Pen of Mercy can ennoble you, and the Merciful One
Can sow in your blindness the seed of Pure Vision.

Be Always Humble

Remember always that all mystic sciences and exercises, all passions and acts of devotion, in comparison with the real worth and majesty of God, are as if someone came to you, bowed once, performed some perfunctory little service, and then went away. If you were to put the entire earth on your heart in serving God, it would be the same as bowing your head once to the ground.

I am not trying to discourage you by saying this, only to instill in you some sense of proportion, some sense of the terrible glory of the One you love.

Do you imagine that God's beauty and worth and magnanimity did not precede your worship and service of them? Wasn't it God who made you able to worship and serve Him? Wasn't it God who gave you some tiny spark of His great passion to love Him with, some tiny flame of His eternal fire of perseverance with which to go on looking for Him? So who are any of us to boast of anything? Anything we can do, anything at all, is like making little forms out of wood and leather and taking them humbly to God, saying, "I love these little forms. I made them; but it is up to You to give them life. Give them life and these my works shall live; if you do not. . . . Everything, everything, is always up to You."

Abraham said, "God is He who gives life and He who makes to die." Nimrod said, "I am He who gives life and makes to die." What arrogance! If God wants, the sun will rise in the west and the mountains will vanish like smoke at one rush of His wind, and all the seas will dissolve in vapor and all the stars fall out of the sky into a pit of eternal darkness. This is the power and this is the infinite majesty and this is the glory of the One we are in love with. Never forget this, or you will be in danger; the path to Him is littered with the bones of those who did not remember Who they were looking for, and how great beyond all concepts and imagining He always is.

The human being is like a sack of corn. The king cries out, "Where are you taking that sack to? My cup is in it."

Most men ignore the cup, never know that it is there, being completely absorbed by the corn.

Every thought or feeling or sudden inner astonishment that draws you toward the invisible world is a reflection of the ray of that cup as its splendor flashes out.

When grace wills it, you will see that world here, you will know this world to be the Rose Garden of rose gardens, a paradise where nothing is ever born and nothing ever dies. You will realize that you and its Gardener are one love, one heart, one breath. This is the heaven He has kept for His lovers; no one arrives in it who has not been through ring after ring of fire.

O King of glory, who needs no drums or banners,
You have made me mad, and madmen live beyond law.
Look at me from a distance, I'm a stumbling fool.
What you see is fantasy only, a mist of nothing.
Step forward yourself now and dare to become nothing.
This nothing I am is the source of the soul;
The real soul, that is, not the one black with grief.
"I" without "I," "you" without "you," together
We'll dive wildly into this burning river;
There's only tyranny and misery on the earth.
You drown in this river, but don't lose your life;
This is the Water of Eternal Life, of grace and mercy.

"My Mystery will always be protected from fools," He said. "For fools think they know, fools think they understand. Fools are never foolish enough to lose their heads for love. And who but the headless ever approach My Throne?"

You say you have seen Him, but your eyes are two stones.
You say you have known Him, but nothing in you trembles.
You still say "I" when you speak of surviving His glory;
No one who has seen It has ever survived.

Freedom, your name is Love! Love, make me your slave!
Slavery to You is the door into the Garden.
My door into eternity is exactly the shape I make
When I walk forward, headless, on my knees.

Man's Search and God's Search

The human search is for something that has not yet been found; day and night human beings search for what they do not yet have. But the search for what has already been found and attained, and yet there is someone looking passionately for that— that is a very strange search indeed, and goes beyond what the human imagination can fathom. Man's search is for something new that he has not yet discovered; his search is for something that has been found already and is then looked for.

The search I am trying to describe is God's search. God has already found everything, and all things are found in His boundless power. "Be, and it is," the Koran says, and names God "the Finder, the Generous." God has indeed found all things, and so is well named the Finder. Yet in spite of all this God is also—and this is the marvelous mystery—the Seeker: "He is the Seeker and the One who vanquishes." What does this mean? "O man, so long as you are swept up in the search that is created in time—which is a human attribute—you find yourself far from the true goal. When your search dies away into God's search and God's searching vanquishes yours, then at last the real search begins. For you are then a seeker by virtue of the search of God Himself."

Stay close, my heart, to the one who knows your ways
Come into the shade of the tree that always has fresh flowers.
Don't stroll idly through the bazaar of the perfume-makers
Stay in the shop of the sugar-seller.
If you don't find true balance, anyone can deceive you;
Anyone can trick out a thing of straw, and make you take it for gold.
Don't squat with a bowl before every boiling pot;
In each pot on the fire you find very different things.
Not all sugarcanes have sugar, not all abysses a peak;
Not all eyes possess vision, not every sea is full of pearls.
O nightingale, with your voice of dark honey! Go on lamenting!
Only your drunken ecstasy can pierce the rock's hard heart!
Surrender yourself, and if you cannot be welcomed by the Friend,
Know that you are rebelling inwardly like a thread
That doesn't want to go through the needle's eye!
The awakened heart is a lamp; protect it by the hem of your robe!
Hurry and get out of this wind, for the weather is bad.
And when you've left this storm, you will come to a fountain;
You'll find a Friend there who will always nourish your soul.
And with your soul always green, you'll grow into a tall tree
Flowering always with sweet light-fruit, whose growth is interior.

Since I Cannot Die, You Must

Two "I"s cannot exist in he presence of God. You say "I," He says "I." Either you will die before Him, or He will die before you, so duality shall not remain. As for God's dying, that is impossible: He is the Eternally Living One, the Deathless, the Immortal. God is so infinitely tender-hearted and so overflowing with grace that if He could die for you so that duality could vanish, He would. But that is impossible. It is up to you to die so He may reveal Himself to you and so that nothing of duality can remain.

Tie two birds together, and although they belong to the same species and have now four wings to fly with, they will not be able to. That is because duality still continues to exist. Tie a dead bird to a living one, and then both can soar easily.

Lovers of the Sun know that the Sun is so loving that it would happily die before the bat. Since this is not in any way possible, the Sun says to the bat, "O bat, My Grace is spread out over all things and all beings, from one end of the horizon to the other, under and along and across all possible worlds. With my whole heart I want to grace you also and make you deathless with My own Splendor. Since I cannot die, you must, so you can share in the Light of My Glory and be transformed from a bat to the immortal bird that lives on My Mountain."

THIRD MOVEMENT

Become
a Lover

There is a window between heart and heart:
They are never separate like two bodies.
Two lamps may not be united in their form–
But their light merges into each other.
No lover ever searched for Union
If his Beloved is not also seeking him.
The love of lovers makes them thin;
The Beloved's love makes them full and shining.
When the lightning of love for the Beloved
Falls from heaven and strikes *this* heart—
Know that love is also firing *that* heart,
And when the love for Him brims over in your heart,
Know that love for you is also brimming in His.
Can the sound of clapping come only from one hand?
When a thirsty man moans, "O water, O delicious water!"
This thirst that is in all our souls
Is the Water drawing us always to It.
We belong to It, and It belongs to us.

Each Moment

Each moment from all sides rushes to us the call to love.
We are running to contemplate its vast green field.
Do you want to come with us?
This is not the time to stay at home
But to go out and give yourself to the Garden.
The dawn of joy has arisen,
And this is the moment of union, of vision.
O king, master of this time, awaken from your drugged sleep.
Straddle the horse of joy, it is here, the moment of our reunion.
The drum of the coming true of promises is beating,
The pathway of heaven is being swept, your joy is now.
What remains for tomorrow is ash.
The horses of day have put to flight the armies of the night,
And heaven and earth are full of the purity of Light.

Our Soul Was Always Drunk on Love

Before any garden or grape or wine existed in this world
Our soul was drunk on eternal wine.
In the Baghdad of pre-eternity, we all proclaimed ecstatically:
"I am the Supreme Reality!"
Long before the scandal and mystery of Mansur Al-Hallaj.

Work for It by Yourself

A man came to Rumi and said, "Please God that I could go
to the other world; there at least I could be at peace because
the Creator is there." "What do you know about where He is?"
answered Rumi. "Everything in all the worlds is in you; whatever
you are hungering for, work for it here by yourself, for you are the
microcosm."

In the Koran it is written: "Wherever you turn, there is the Face
    of God."
That "Face" extends on all sides, forever and ever.
Real lovers sacrifice themselves
For the sake of that Face, and look for no reward.

Love is an infinite Sea whose skies are a bubble of foam.
Know that it is the waves of Love that turn the wheels of Heaven,
Without Love, nothing in the world would have life.
How is an inorganic thing transformed into a plant?
How are plants sacrificed to become rich with spirit?
How is spirit sacrificed to become Breath,
One scent of which is potent enough to make Mary pregnant?
Every single atom is drunk on this Perfection and runs towards It
And what does this running secretly say but "Glory be to God!"

Him, for Himself Alone

Everything in this world—wealth, a wife, fine clothes, status, power of any and every kind—is destined for something other than itself. Even if you had a huge heap of money and were hungry and couldn't find anything to eat, you wouldn't be able to eat the money. A wife is for love and children, and to satisfy desire. Clothes are to keep out the cold.

God and God alone is desired for His own sake. Since He is better, higher and nobler, and more subtle than all other things, how could He possibly be desired for anything less than Himself? When you have reached God, you have reached everything—your Self, the worlds, and everything, everywhere. When you have attained God, you have attained the ultimate goal, the goal that nothing transcends.

Look into yourself once honestly, and you will see that the human soul is a bloody arena of doubts, difficulties, and gross and subtle forms of suffering. The only way of being clear of all these is to be truly and completely in love.

Day has come, dragging tumult with it;
Night has come, firing the two worlds with passion.
This isn't the day or night's business; it's mine—
How could two crippled donkeys carry my glory?

Listen to the reed. Listen to how it tells a story.
And listen to how it complains of separation, saying:
"Ever since I was parted from the reed-bed,
My lament has caused both men and women to mourn.
I want a bosom and a breast that is torn by separation,
So I may unfold fully the pain of the desire of the heart."
Everyone who is left far from his source
Longs to return to the time when he was united with it.
The noise of the reed I am talking about is fire, not wind.
Anyone who isn't possessed by this fire will be annihilated.
It is the fire of love that is in the reed,
It is the fervor of love that is in the wine.
The reed is the friend of everyone
Who has been parted from a friend.
Its strains pierce our heart.
Whoever saw a poison, or a cure, like the reed?
Whoever saw a consoler and a longing lover like the reed?
The reed tells stories of the passion of Majnun,
Only to the senseless is this sense confided.

If you have lost heart in the Path of Love
Flee to Me without delay—
I am a fortress invincible.

Love's creed is separate from all religions. The belief and denomi-
nation of lovers is God.

My religion is to live through love.

If you have not been a lover, count not your life as lived;
On the Day of Reckoning, it will not be counted.

Never live without love, or you will be dead. Die with love and you
will remain alive.

Love is the bottomless ocean of life; eternal life the least of its gifts.

Always Be a Lover

Wherever you may be, in whatever situation or circumstance you may find yourself, strive always to be a lover, and a passionate lover. Once you possess your heart in love, you will always be a lover, in the tomb, at the Resurrection, and in Paradise forever and ever.

Sow wheat and wheat will grow; wheat will flourish in the fields, and bread will glow in the oven.

Majnun wanted to send a letter to Layla. He seized a pen and wrote:

> *Your name is on my tongue*
> *Your image haunts my sight*
> *Your memory fills my heart*
> *So where can I write?*

Your image lives in my eyes, your name is never away from my tongue. Your memory fills the depths of my soul, so where am I to write a letter, since you are everywhere and in all things? His pen broke and the page was torn.

There are many people whose hearts are brimming with love; yet, although they are real lovers, they can't express themselves. This isn't surprising and presents no obstacle on the Quest; what matters is the state of the heart, its longing and passion. A child loves the milk its mother feeds it and draws vigor and help from it; yet a child cannot define milk or express love of it, saying, "What joy I get from drinking milk! How feeble and distressed I become when I am not drinking it." His whole soul might be on fire for milk but still he couldn't say anything about it. He accepts the milk, drinks it, and smiles. The joy on his face is all his mother wants.

The Heart Always Loves

In every circumstance and situation, the heart is drunk on the Beloved, occupied only with adoration of Him. The heart has no need to travel the various stages of the Path; it is the place-less place where He lives already, and the love it loves Him with is a spark of the Fire of His own Passion. There is a rope of light between your heart and His that nothing can weaken or break, and it is always in His hands. The heart never needs to fear ambush from bandits; the heart does not need a horse and saddle and provisions and a complicated map. It is the body that needs—and is chained to—these things.

I said to my heart, "How, my heart,
Can you be so crazy
As to swerve from the service
Of the One you bless?"

My heart replied, "It is you who are mad
To see me wrongly—
I am always in His service,
It is you that stray."

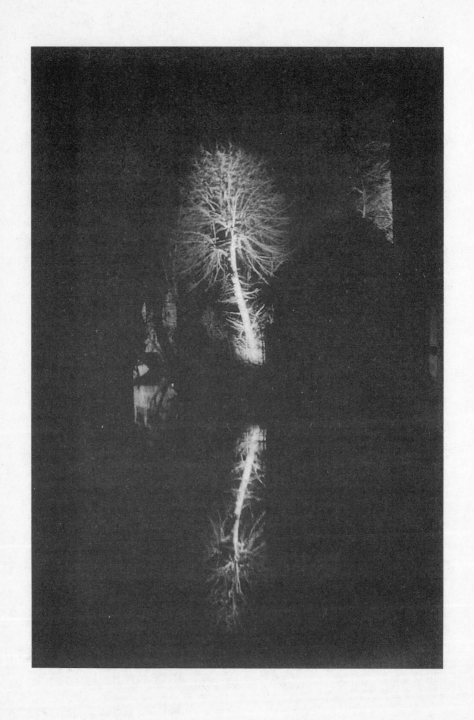

Joseph and the Mirror

A friend of Joseph's came to visit him after returning from a long journey. "What present have your brought me?" Joseph asked. "What could I bring you," his friend replied, "that you don't already have?" "But," he added, "because you are so beautiful, and nothing exists in all the worlds more beautiful than you, I have brought you a mirror, so you can know the joy at every moment of seeing your own face."

Is there anything that God doesn't have already that you could give Him? Is there anything that God could need that you could possibly provide? All you are here for, and the entire meaning of the Path of Love, is to bring before God a heart bright as a mirror, so God can see His own face in it.

Tomorrow you'll be brave, you say? Fool! Dive today
From the cliff of what you know into what you can't know.
You fear the rocks? Better men than you have died on them;
Dying on Love's rocks is nobler than a life of death.

You're the Emperor of wonder, my God!
You're the peace and flame of my soul, my God!
Every morning, before Your Face, in rapture,
The sun of this world stammers: "My God!"

Make of your heart a sacrifice, so it can awaken to My Sacrifice
Make of your heart a furnace, so it can know My Conflagration
Make of your heart a diamond, so I can set it in my Crown
So the Lights from my Throne can enter you and make you King.

One Thing

In reality, what attracts you is one thing, however million-formed it may appear. Think of someone simultaneously possessed by what seems like one hundred different demands. "I want spaghetti. I want tripe. I want chips. I want steak tartar. I want dates and fruit and sardines and those little crabs you find off the coast in Izmar and the first spring broccoli," and so on. He may name all the things he wants, describe them in pedantic precision; the root of the whole business is a single thing: "hunger." And when he has eaten his fill of one of the things he demands, he won't want any of the others! It wasn't ten thousand different things that was attracting him, but one. The Koran says, "And their number we have made only as a trial"—or a trial to see if you can understand what I have been saying, which is what all true lovers discover. There is one Love, one Sun shining in and through all things; all desires are desires for That.

Whatever inspires the mind is of the perfume of my Beloved,
Whatever fires the heart is a ray from my Friend.

Whatever you love here in existence
Has been gold-plated by God's qualities;
When that gold goes back to Origin
Only a dull copper will remain,
And you will be disgusted and reject it.
Don't go on calling counterfeit coin "beautiful"
That beauty you love is only borrowed.
Gold will abandon all surfaces in the end
And return to the Mine of Magnificence.
Why not set out for that Mine?
The light will return from the wall to the sun;
Go now to that Sun that dances always in harmony.
From now on, take your water from heaven directly
Why go on trusting a rusting drainpipe?

Like cream concealed in the heart of milk,
No-place keeps seeping into place.
Like intellect hidden in this sack of blood,
The Traceless keeps infiltrating traces.
From beyond the intellect, astounding Love arrives
Dragging its robes, a cup of wine in its hand.
And from beyond Love, that Indescribable One
Who can only be called "That" keeps coming and coming.

What do I know if I exist or not?
This is all I know, my Beloved:
When I exist, I am non-existent;
When I am non-existent, I exist!

When a miracle turns its face toward the Realm of Plants
Life flowers from the tree of its great good fortune.
And when a plant tastes grace and turns to the Spirit
It drinks its fill from the Fountain of Spring.
And when the spirit turns at last toward its Beloved
It unrolls its bed in Eternal Delight.

Make real the sublime words of the Prophet:
"We are the last and the foremost."
The fresh and perfect fruit is the last thing to come into
    existence
For although the fruit is the last thing to come into
    existence,
It is, in fact, the first, for it was the goal.

Love cannot be contained within "speaking" or "listening"
Love is a Sea whose depths cannot be fathomed.
Would you dare try and count the drops of the sea?
Before the Sea of Love, the seven seas are nothing.

What is our "we" if You once say "I"?
Can copper withstand the philosopher's stone?
Before Your Sun, what can a ball of snow do
But be annihilated forever in radiance and light?

God said to Love: "If it wasn't for Your Beauty
Why would I pay attention to the mirror of existence?"
To the ones who really see, the Chosen Lovers,
Love is a shattering Eternal Light.

At the time of separation, Love creates imaginary forms
When Union arrives, the Formless One appears,
Saying "I am the Origin of the origin of sobriety and wine;
Beauty in all its forms is a reflection of Me.
Now, this moment, I withdraw all veils to reveal
Beauty's final splendor, without any intermediary.
For so long now you have been busy with My reflection—
You have won the power now to gaze at My Essence alone."

Can anyone really describe the actions of the Matchless One?
Anything I can say is only what I'm allowed to.
Sometimes He acts this way, sometimes in its exact opposite;
The real work of religion is permanent astonishment.
By that I don't mean in astonishment turning your back on
    Him—
I mean: blazing in blind ecstasy, drowned in God and drunk
    on Love.

You Are My Soul

You are my soul, my universe: what do I have
    to do with the soul and the universe?
For me you are ever-flowing treasure; what do I have
    to do with profit or loss?
One minute I am the friend of the wine, another the
    friend of him who burns me.
I have come to this age of ruins, so what do I have to
    do with time's melodrama?
I am terrified by the whole world, I am sprung free of
    the whole world,
I am neither "hidden" nor "apparent." What do I
    have to do with existence or space?
I am drunk on union with you, I need and want and
    care about no one else.
Since I am your prey, what do I care about fate's bow
    and its arrows?
I live at the bottom of the stream, why would I go
    looking for water?
What could or would I say about this stream that
    flows and flows?
I have given up existence, why go on staggering under
    the burden of this mountain?
Since the wolf is my shepherd, why put up with the
    pretensions of the shepherd?
What abandon! What drunkenness! You hold the cup
    in your hand.
Blessed is the place you are, and glorious to the eye of
    the heart.
Each atom, by your grace, is a universe, each drop of
    water a soul.

No one who has ever had a sign from you need worry
    again about "name" or "sign."
To find the place of splendor, at the bottom of the sea of truths,
You have to dive, dive head first; what do I have to do
    with feet that scurry?
With the sword of the One God you have hacked a
    Path for us;
You have stolen all my clothes; what will I give to the
    toll-man?
From your beauty ablaze like the sun, from the curls
    of your hair,
My heart has become ecstatic; O my soul, hand me
    this brimming cup,
Do not weigh pain and misery, contemplate love,
    contemplate friendship;
Do not mull over tyranny and neglect; think of all
    those who have their eyes fixed on you.
Surname all grief "grace"; transmute pain and
    anguish into joy,
And ask from joy all happiness, all security, all peace.
Demand that security, that peace, demand them,
Choose the company of those withdrawn in love.
Listen to those who open a path to you: listen, and
    don't say a word.

Love's Poverty

The way of Love's Poverty is a way where you get every-
thing you want. On this way, whatever you have longed for
will undoubtedly be given to you—whether it be victory over your
enemies, becoming greater than your contemporaries, elegance of
speech, visionary eloquence—anything at all that your being really
hungers for.

When you have wholly and sincerely taken the way of Love's
Poverty, then all these things come to you. No one has ever taken
this way and had anything at all to regret. Take any other path in
life and you will find that out of a thousand enticing goals it
promises, you will realize at most only one or two; all other ways,
however seductive they seem, conceal disillusion.

When you have wholly given yourself to the Way of Poverty,
God will give you worlds and kingdoms you never imagined, and
you will weep with shame and embarrassment at what you wanted
before. "With such glories to find and live here," you will say to
yourself, "how could I have wanted such meager joys?" God will
say to you, "If you had been able to not want these things it would
have been better. Nevertheless, when the passion for them arose
in you, you curbed and abandoned it for My sake. My Love is infi-
nite, so I now give to you what you gave up for Me."

When the Prophet first met the Arabs, he longed to have their
elegance and eloquence. When the invisible world opened its door
to him and he grew drunk on its splendor, he was disgusted with
himself and gave up that longing. Then God said to him, "I am going
to give you the elegance and eloquence you so wanted." Mohammed
replied, "Lord, what use would they be to me? I do not want them
now; I am indifferent to them." God replied, "Because you are indif-
ferent to them, you will now receive them and not be harmed by
them. Do not worry. And do not be afraid." And God graced
Mohammed such a power of speech that the whole world has been

shaken to its foundations by it, and people are still writing book after book trying to describe some of its effects, and no one understands its magnificence completely. God also said to Mohammed, "Your companions used to keep your name secret to protect you from the jealous. I will make it famous through the world and see that men call it from every minaret."

Anyone who gambles away his life on this path will, like the Prophet, be rewarded beyond his dreams. All his goals—secular or spiritual—will be attained by him through the grace of Love, and in such a way that pride and ambition cannot sear him or make him prisoner. And he will rejoice in his inner and outer health and prosperity, humbly and without any vanity, knowing who is furnishing and sustaining them, and with what lavish tenderness. His heart, polished by praise and gratitude, will become an ever-clearer mirror in which the Face can appear more and more brilliantly, streaming ever-richer graces and transforming powers into the core of his heart and life.

And so he will come to know the secret name of the Way of Poverty; that is, the Way of Infinite Treasure.

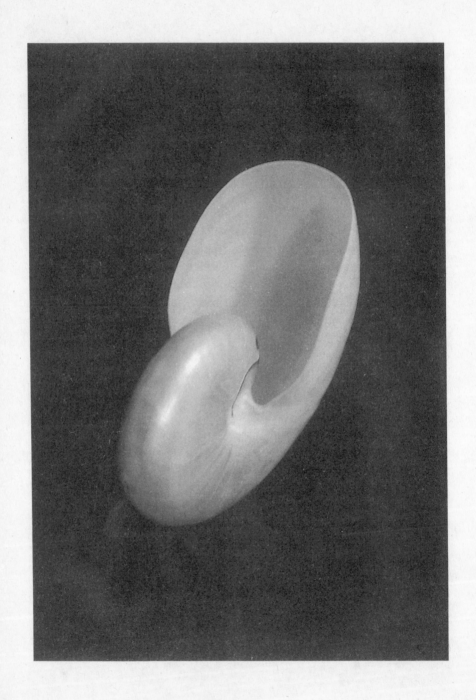

The Pearl

If you could attain everything I am talking about just by listening, no one would ever need to strive and pray and labor night and day for the Treasure. There would be no need for the thousands of small sacrifices and efforts that are essential for purification and the polishing of the heart.

A man arrives at the sea and sees nothing but saltwater, fishes, and shark-fins. "Where is this so-called Pearl they go on about?" he says. "They must be lying." Does this idiot imagine that you could win such a Pearl simply by staring at the sea? Even if he were to take a cup and measure out the sea in a million, million cupfuls, he would still never find the Pearl. To discover the Pearl, you need a diver. Not any diver will do—you need a diver who is both skilled and lucky.

All metaphysics and theology—all kinds of knowledge, in fact, and all the arts—are like measuring the sea with a cup. To find the Pearl demands a wholly different attitude.

I have met people who are beautiful, intelligent, rich, and gracious, who seem to have everything, but who lack the mysterious sincerity essential for the Path. And I have met people who seemed to be wrecks and have nothing—neither elegance nor beauty nor attractive intelligence—and yet the Pearl sat in the palm of their hands, because Love was in their hearts, and in its full passion.

The passionate and all-consuming love of God is the Immortal Element within us, and with its courage and skill we can find the Pearl. Without it, we may find and own everything else. But what are other jewels to the Pearl? All worlds and heavens together are worth far less than It, being just passing shadows of its Eternal Luster.

He who perceives Your chain-like, linked tress-on-tress and then
stays "rational" is mad.

Mad desire for Desire and the Water of Life makes Love enflame
A thousand thousand fires and furnaces every second.

When someone comes in and boasts "It is I,"
Immediately, I beat him fiercely about the head—
"This is the Mosque of Love, you animal, not a stable!"

Whatever form you can imagine, He stands above it
Like a painter above his brush.
However much "higher" you gaze, He is higher
    than that "higher"!
Abandon words, abandon books—let Him be your Book!

Make Real My Words in Surrender

The words I am speaking are like a beautiful bride: if a beautiful woman is bought just to be sold again, how can she love her buyer or fix her passion on him? All the pleasure of her buyer comes not from loving but from selling, and so he might as well be impotent; he buys the bride only to sell her again, and doesn't have the courage or virility to buy her for himself.

If a perfect Indian sword came into the possession of a hermaphrodite, he would only sell it. If a Pehlevi bow also fell into his hands, a bow of the most rare quality, he would sell that too; he wouldn't have the strength to draw the bow himself. All he wants the bow for is its valuable string; he hasn't the power or skill himself to use that string. And when he does sell the bow, what does he buy with the money? Rouge, indigo, and cheap perfume.

Don't say smugly, "I understand what you are saying." The more you imagine yourself to have "understood," the more mired in ignorance you become. Understanding what I am saying lies in not understanding. Everything that troubles you and makes you miserable comes from your "understanding." That "understanding" is an airless prison for you; do anything to escape from it, if you want to be anything in life.

It is as if you said, "I tried to fill my sheepskin from the sea and the sea did not fit in it." This would be crazy talk, of course. Much wiser to say, "My sheepskin was lost in the sea"—that would be real, humble, noble, and the whole root of the matter. Reason is worthy and wonderful until it brings you to the door of the King. When you have reached the door, divorce reason for good; at this point it can only do you harm and be a malicious bandit of love.

When you have come into the Presence of the King and start to feel the majesty of His Glory and His Love, you have only one thing to do: surrender to Him and go on and on surrendering more and more of yourself to Him with more and more faith, trust, joy, and deeper and deeper inner security. You have no use now for reason's smart distinctions and formulas, for its clever "what" and "how" and "why." Your duty now is love, more and more surrender and more and more love, and not only in this body and this world but in all the bodies and worlds to come, forever.

Adoration is the key to evolution on the Path of Love, and that evolution can never end, because Love is infinite and so is the transforming power that streams from it. God is drawing the universe—all the universes—continually closer to Him through spiral after spiral of Adoration. Open your heart and know: the expansion of the heart is infinite.

This Love sacrifices all souls, however wise, however "awakened."
Cuts off their heads without a sword, hangs them without a
　　scaffold.
We are the guests of the One who devours His guests,
The friends of the One who slaughters His friends.
Although by His gaze He brings death to so many lovers
Let yourself be killed by Him: is He not the water of life?
Never, ever, grow bitter; He is the friend and kills gently.
Keep your heart noble, for this most noble love
Kills only kings near God and those free from passion.
We are like the night, earth's shadow.
He is the Sun: He splits open the night with a sword soaked
　　in dawn.

The man to whom is unveiled the mystery of Love
Exists no longer, but vanishes into Love.
Place before the Sun a burning candle
And watch its brilliance disappear before that blaze.
The candle exists no longer, it is transformed into Light;
There are no more signs of it, it itself becomes sign.

The heavens cannot contain Me, or the void,
Or winged exalted intelligences, or souls;
Yet I am contained, as a guest, in the heart of the true believer.
And without any qualification, definition, or description,
From this blazing mirror, every second, spring
Fifty wedding feasts for the spirit.

Give Up Childish Games

Husam al-Din Arzanjani was a formidable debater before he became a Sufi. Wherever he went, he loved to engage in controversy. He was brilliant and spoke with furious eloquence. But then Love came and cut off his head, and he gave up in shame those petty games.

> It takes another Love
> The death of one to give.

When a person has become adult, he or she no longer plays childish games. If they do, they do it secretly. Intellectual knowledge and discussion are like wind, and human beings are like dust. When wind whips up dust, wherever it goes it only makes eyes weep with irritation. Nothing but distress and confusion springs from it.

But when instead of wind the Water of Love, of Life, of Grace, of Wonder, showers down upon the dust, then the opposite happens. Where there was only sterile dirt, fruit and grass and perfumed herbs and roses and violets all laugh and flourish.

The Drama of Reason

Reason can never understand the love of Love, can never dance in the incandescent madness of vision, can never become lucid through the drunkenness of ecstasy. Yet reason can never completely give up the desire to understand Love, otherwise it would stop being reason. What is reason but that faculty within us that is always restless night and day, thinking and fighting and scheming and struggling horribly to understand and schematize and control?—even though He is always uncomprehended, uncontrollable, and, by any human or angelic intelligence, forever incomprehensible.

Reason is condemned, then, to participate in a hilarious and terrible Divine Game. Reason is like a moth and He, the Beloved, the Mine of Love and Vision and Ecstasy and true mystical Wisdom, is like a blazing candle. Whenever the moth, in its abject, driven longing to penetrate the flame that haunts it, dashes itself against the candle it is burned, consumed, annihilated. But the nature of the moth is that however many times it is seared and devoured it cannot bear for one moment to live without the candle. If there were an insect like the moth that could not live without the candle flame, it would itself be a moth; and if the moth ran into the flame and was not consumed, that would not be a candle.

The person who can do without God is not really a human being at all; if he were able to understand God, God would not be God. God is the One who burns all human beings away and makes them Nothing; God is the One whom no reason can ever comprehend. Only Love can know Love, and why should Love stand back and watch and assess, when it can blaze and dance?

Lovers and men of intellect cannot mix;
How can you mix the broken with the unbroken?
Cautious men of intellect shrink back from a dead ant;
Lovers, completely carefree, trample down dragons.

The intellect says: "The six directions are limits: there
    is no way out."
Love says: "There is a way. I have traveled it
    thousands of times."
The intellect saw a market and started to haggle;
Love saw thousands of markets beyond that market.
Lovers who drink the dregs of the wine reel from bliss
    to bliss;
The dark-hearted men of reason
Burn inwardly with denial.
The intellect says: "Do not go forward, annihilation
    contains only thorns."
Love laughs back: "The thorns are in you."
Enough words! Silence!
Pull the thorn of existence out of the heart! Fast!
For when you do, you will see thousands of rose
    gardens in yourself.

In the howling storm of Love
What is the intellect but a gnat?

The partial intellect cannot but deny love;
Even when it boasts, it understands its mysteries.
It is adroit and nimble-witted, but not annihilated.
As long as an angel is not annihilated, it is a devil.

Since intelligence only incites you to pride and vanity
Become a fool, so your heart stays pure.
Not a fool who wastes his life in playing the idiot,
But a fool who is lost and astounded in Him.
If, through astonishment, your reason leaps out
    of your head,
Every hair on your head will become a new head,
Every hair on your head will become a new intellect.

On Love and Universal Intellect

Love will initiate you into the Universal Intellect, and teach you by stages how to drown your reason in its fire-eyed wonder and precision.

Mohammed was called "illiterate" not because he could not read or write. He was called "illiterate" for a much higher reason, because with him reading and writing were innate and sprang from Origin and were not acquired. A being who can write on the face of the moon can hardly be called "illiterate." What in all the world does the Prophet not know, since the whole world learns from him? What could belong to the partial intellect that the Universal Intellect does not possess?

Men in the partial intellect borrow obsessively, and repeat and repeat. The people who invent something new invent it with Love's freshness and creativity, and so with the Universal Intellect. In fact, they *are* the Universal Intellect. The partial intellect can learn and needs to be taught; the Universal Intellect teaches and has no need to learn anything.

Investigate any skill or profession and you'll discover that the root of them all is Revelation; people learned them from prophets and saints and holy beings, who are the Universal Intellect.

Remember the story of the raven. When Cain killed Abel, he did not know what to do. A raven killed another raven and dug the soil with its beak and covered it with earth. From this Cain leaned how to make a grave and how to bury. It is the same with every skill. The Universal Intellect is the founder of everything, and it is the saints and prophets and mystics who have married the partial intellect and the Universal Intellect so that they are one.

The body is crude compared to the subtlety of the mind and heart. The grass continues to live through the subtle and unseen; if it has any vividness or freshness, it gets them from the subtle, and without the subtle it is useless, foul, and dead. So the partial intellect in comparison with the Universal Intellect is only a tool that learns from It and is instructed by It, a dead thing in comparison to that Fountain of Endless Life.

Love will interpret these words to you and reveal the kernel of their mystery, if you dare to allow it. Don't be lazy and just take my word for it; when you look at a train of camels it is easy to tell which of the camels are in rut: their eyes stream, they walk differently, they foam at the mouth. As the Koran says, "Their mark is on their faces, the sear-mark of prostration."

That is the mark I am scanning your face and eyes for. When it is there, I know I do not have to say anything: you already know. But we talk for the joy of worship, and our hearts smile.

Only Love, Only Love

The Prophet said that Abu Bakr's superiority over others was not due to more prayer, or more fasting, or more devotional works, but because God's special grace was with him in the form of the immensity of *his* love for God. On Resurrection Day when people's prayers are called forward, they will be placed in a balance along with their fasts, their works of charity, their fine intentions; but when Love is summoned, no balance could be found that could ever contain It. The essence of the whole matter is Love.

So I beg you: whenever you detect Love growing awake in you, feed It so it may open Its eyes further. When you see that the passion for God is in your heart, increase it by questing deeper and wilder, for "In movement there is blessing." If you do not aspire and struggle to increase it, it will dwindle. Are you less than earth? Don't people turn the earth with hoes to make it yield crops? If they leave it be, doesn't the soil quickly grow hard and infertile?

When you feel the Quest hot inside you, set out, be always in fervent movement. Don't ask why, don't make bargains, keep moving and the reason will appear of itself, attended by many graces and visions and expanded possibilities. You go into a shop, don't you, and simply say what you need. God gives and provides everything; if you sit glumly or smugly at home, pretending to be self-sufficient, then what you need cannot come to you.

Think of a baby. It cries, and its mother gives it milk. If it were to think, "What use is there in my crying?" or, worse still, "What is the cause and meaning of her giving me milk?" the child would never get any milk. It cries: the milk arrives. Divine laws are simpler than human ones—which is why it can take a lifetime to be able to understand them. Only Love can understand them, as only Love can interpret these words as they are meant to be interpreted. Only Love, only Love, only Love—how many times must I repeat it before you leap into the fire?

Sit with Lovers

Lovers know miseries and strange forms of anguish that nothing, nothing at all, can cure—neither sleeping, nor travel, nor fame, nor money, nor eating—only the sight and presence of the Beloved. It is said, "Meet the Friend and your illness will end." This is so true that even if a hypocrite sits down in a throng of believers, their fervor will rub off on him and he will find himself starting to become a believer. God says in the Koran: "When people of this kind meet real believers, they say, 'We believe.'"

What an alchemy is begun, then, when a believer sits down with a fellow believer! If being with believers transforms hypocrites, imagine what it does for sincere lovers of God! When wool meets a gifted carpet maker, it becomes a miracle of rich design; earth in the hands of skilled bricklayers and architects can become a thousand-windowed palace. If the society of gifted beings so transfigures inanimate things, imagine how the society of a real believer can infuse and inspire another one!

Drunkards who want to stay drunk drink with other seasoned debauchees; mystics who want to keep their hearts fiery and their minds absorbed should see that they associate as much as possible with other lovers. Better to be alone than with the rational and sober; their minds are winter, and shrivel the mystic's exuberance. Do not hate the sober; pray that one day love may seize and make them human, but protect yourself as resourcefully as you can from them. I have sometimes found them surprisingly vicious, these sober-seeming, calmly smiling rationalists who think they can explain everything and yet are jealous of the Lover's splendor.

How confining the sober are to those who have known the Vision of Wine! How dead their reasonings seem to be to those who drown repeatedly in their heart-blood! How ugly rings the metallic music of their certainties! How brutal are their meticulous yet entirely illusory and self-satisfying formulas! God is Beauty, and nothing about them is beautiful; God is Splendor, and nothing about them is splendid; God is Magnanimous, and nothing about them is magnanimous; God is Fire, and nothing about them is incandescent. They believe they rule the world, unaware that what they rule is a heap of ash that one breath of the Beloved could disperse forever. When they anger you, or threaten to drive you to despair, imagine their faces when at the Resurrection they see the mountains turn into smoke and the heavens peel away like paper!

Avoid them—politely, compassionately, serenely—but avoid them.

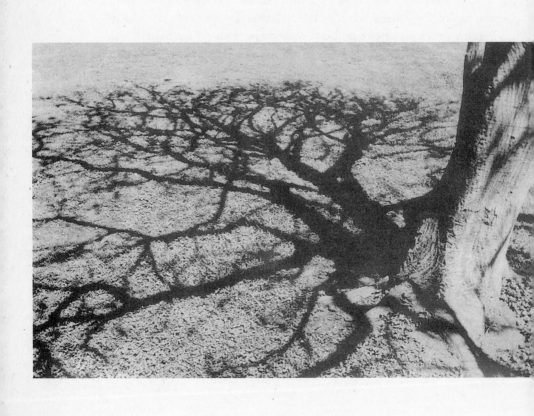

Trembling and Passionate Love

Many simply don't have the stamina to bear Presence, and prefer absence. They like to feel from a distance the warmth of the Fire, not risking to walk and dance in it. The day's shining springs entirely from the Sun—but many, many eyes just can't stand gazing fierce and eagle-like into the Sun's heart. Better for people like this to keep calmly busy at some useful task or another; they are not made to be Sun-starers. Talking about tasty dishes to a sick person might stimulate his appetite and encourage him to build his strength—but actually putting such dishes before him would only make him more ill.

Trembling, passionate love is necessary in the Quest for God. Anyone who hasn't yet learned how to tremble must wait for someone who has to teach him or inspire him.

Have you noticed that no fruit ever ripens on the trunk of a tree? Trunks never tremble; branches do, their tips especially. The trunk's sacred task is to strengthen the branches so they can bear fruit safely—the fruit that also keeps the trunk itself safe from the axe. If its trunk did tremble, the whole tree would be a ruin, so it is best that trunks stay stock-still. This is how they can serve their trembling, fertile branches as nobly as possible.

God Does It

An emperor ordered each of his slaves to pick up a golden cup; he was about to receive someone he loved and wanted to do him honor. He ordered his favorite slave also to pick up a cup. However, when the emperor appeared, his favorite, on seeing him, lost all control of his senses and became crazed by his beauty, and the golden cup tumbled from his hand and was broken into a thousand pieces.

The other slaves saw this, and imitative in everything, thought to themselves, "Because he did it, we should do the same." So they threw down their cups and smashed them.

The emperor was furious. "Why did you do that?!" he thundered.

"Because your favorite did."

"You fools," cried the emperor, "*he* didn't do it. *I* did."

The Veils Are Necessary

All desires are the desire for God, obscured and veiled. When you go out of this world and see the King face-to-face then you will know that everything you longed for here—whether women or men, wealth or palaces, things to eat, political or religious power—all these things were veils and coverings of Him. You will see, beyond doubt, that you were only always looking for Him. All difficulties will then dissolve; you will hear in the silence of your astonished heart the answers to all questions and the resolutions to all problems, and everything will be seen and known directly.

God's way is not to answer each question or difficulty laboriously, one by one, like some pedantic schoolmaster. His way is to give one overwhelming answer that sweeps away forever all doubts and agony. In winter a man puts on a warm cloak and shelters himself from the wind in a warm place. Plants and trees also hide their wealth inwardly so the winter cannot destroy them. When in a single epiphany spring answers all their questions, all their problems, however different they may superficially seem, whether they are alive, flourishing, ugly, or lying dormant—all of them drown and die at once in spring's flood of green truth. All plants and trees will flower again and realize what was the root of their desolation.

God did not create these thousands of veils between us and Him without any reason. If God's beauty and wild majesty were to flame out in wave after wave of blinding lightning without any veil, no one could endure them. The veils between Him and us enable Him, in His tenderness, to sustain and nourish us as we are.

Think of the sun. We walk in its light, and tell by it the difference between good and bad, and are fed by it. By it, orchards and fields are made fruitful; in its mellow heat their fruits, that begin unripe and sour, gather slowly the sweet, full juice that will ripen them and make them perfect. Through its power veins of gold and silver and rubies and carnelian are created and revealed. If this sun, which through its intermediaries and veils give us so much and enriches our lives in so many subtle and marvelous ways, were to come closer to the earth, the whole world and all its creatures would be burned to a crisp. Everything we know and love would be annihilated.

When God reveals himself veiled to a mountain, the mountain laughs and is covered with grasses and flowering trees and rosebushes that inebriate the birds and attract them and make the mountain a garden of birdsong.

If God, however, were to reveal himself to the mountain without a veil, it would be as if he crumpled it in His Fist of Light, tore it apart atom by atom and flung each atom in different directions down into the deepest darkness and nothingness.

The Koran tells us:

> "His Lord revealed to him the Mountain
> And made it in a moment dissolve into dust."

Love's Touch

How many thousands of times have you planned something and your plans came to nothing? But then you forget, don't you, and plan and plot again, as if you were the master of your destiny! This obliviousness of the past is also God's magic. As the Koran says: "God stands between a man and his heart."

What does the Lover learn? That "the heart is between two fingers of the All-Merciful." God turns us all effortlessly between His fingers; the Lover's reward for surrender is to feel the tenderness of that Touch.

Ibrahim was a king and went out hunting. He galloped after a deer, leaving his fellow hunters behind. His horse was sweaty and exhausted but, driven by a strange impulse, Ibrahim galloped on and on. When he had totally lost his way, the deer started to speak. It turned its head back toward him and addressed him: "You were not created miraculously out of nothing just to be a hunter. Even if you do catch me, what good will that do you?"

The words pierced Ibrahim's heart and he cried out and flung himself from his horse onto the ground. A shepherd happened to be passing by. Ibrahim begged him, "Take my jeweled clothes, take my horse, take my weapons, and give me in exchange your coarse robe and never tell anyone ever what has happened to me." He put on the shepherd's rough cloth and went on the path of his real destiny.

He had wanted to hunt and catch the deer—that was his plan—but God hunted him and caught him through the deer.

In this world and in all others, everything happens by His Will, and for purposes hidden in Mystery.

Love, and Love only, will lead you to the placeless place where you know this simply, and so smile inwardly and fear no more.

Love's World

 Adore and love Him with your whole being, and He will reveal to you that each thing in the universe is a vessel full to the brim with wisdom and beauty. Each thing he will show you is one drop from the boundless river of His Infinite Beauty. He will take away the veil that hides the splendor of each thing that exists, and you will see that each thing is a hidden treasure because of its divine fullness, and you will know that each thing has already exploded stilly and silently and made the earth more brilliant than any heaven. At His summoning, all things have sprung up and made the earth more magnificent than an emperor wearing a robe of the most resplendent satin.

If you could see the ugliest leper with the eyes of Love,
His beauty would out-dazzle in your eyes the starlit sea.
If one drop of the Wine of Vision could rinse your eyes,
Wherever you looked, you would weep with wonder.

That Door

What a terrible and magnificent magician God is! He creates forms of sumptuous beauty that hide in their core horrible and evil forms. Why? So that no one can say in the craziness of pride, "A wonderful idea and action took form in me and then I performed marvels."

You hear this, and nod wisely. Do you know what is going to happen tomorrow or in the next moment? Do you know who is your real friend or your secret enemy? Do you know the hour of your death? Do you know the real names of every one of the angels? Do you know what transforms a stone into a plant? Do you know from what fountain Love springs? Seeing how little any of us know, or can know, or ever will or could know, inwardly remain always on your knees.

A man once asked me, "Is there a way into the Other Place here on earth?" I said, "Yes, there is a door between this room and the Other. For every person its size is subtly different, for it has the shape each being makes when on their knees."

No one enters the Rose Garden unless lost in adoration and wonder; no one walks through *that* door except on their knees.

The Real Step

The rumor of a great lion spread throughout the world. A man wanted to see the lion and for a year endured all the hardships of the journey and traveled from place to place. When he arrived at the forest and saw the lion from a distance, he came to a sudden halt. He couldn't move and couldn't go any further.

Someone who knew the lion said to the man gently, "You've come such a long way out of love for the lion. Know this about him: if you go toward him bravely and tenderly stroke him, he will not harm you in any way; if you are afraid, he will be furious. Sometimes he even attacks people who are scared of him, howling, 'How dare you have such a black opinion of me!' You've endured a year of bitter difficulty to get here to see him. Why are you standing still now that you are so close? Take one more step toward him!"

No one could find in themselves the courage to advance even one step. Everyone said, "Every step we took before this was easy. Here, we cannot move."

It takes immense faith to take one step toward the Lion in the presence of the Lion. That step is a majestic and noble act, one that only the Elect and Friends of God are capable of. This is the real step on the Path; all the other steps are just vanishing footprints. And the faith required to take it comes only to saints and prophets, to those who have washed their hands of their own life.

Only the supremely brave ever admit
How helpless they are in the hands of God!
As for the others, building and decorating
    their sandcastles—
Look how one wild wave shatters them all.

To Enjoy This Conversation

I must tell you something now or mislead you. And I would rather die than mislead you on this Path that is so beautiful and so hard. A false step can mean death or madness or futility or the destruction of years of hard-won attainment.

What I want to tell you is that all of these words I speak, out of love and inspiration and whatever knowledge God has graced me with, are for the sake of the person who needs words in order to understand. As for the person who understands without words, obviously he or she doesn't need words at all. In fact, to the one who really understands, the heavens and the earth themselves are "words"; after all; they came into being through "words"—the Divine Words "Be! And it is." If someone can hear a low, subtle whisper, is there any need to shout and scream?

Make everything in you an ear, each atom of your being, and you will hear at every moment what the Source is whispering to you, just to you and for you, without any need for my words or anyone else's. You are—we all are—the beloved of the Beloved, and in every moment, in every event of your life, the Beloved is whispering to you exactly what you need to hear and know. Who can ever explain this miracle? It simply is. Listen and you will discover it every passing moment. Listen, and your whole life will become a conversation in thought and act between you and Him, directly, wordlessly, now and always.

It was to enjoy this conversation that you and I were created.

On True Absorption

When the heart is completely absorbed, all the other faculties of the body and spirit are annihilated in it, and there is no need of talk. Think of Layla: she was just a flesh-and-blood woman, but Majnun's passion for her so possessed him that he had no need to see her with his eyes, or hear her voice, because never for a moment did he see Layla apart from himself. He had become one with her beyond space and time and any form of separation, gross or subtle.

You can see from this just how potent physical passion can be—so potent that it can conjure a man into the state where he never sees himself apart from the one he loves. All of Majnun's senses were drowned and absorbed in Layla. No faculty sought any other satisfaction, seeing and finding its consummation in adoration of Layla. If one of his senses were to seek some other kind of joy, that would show that that sense had not sat down at the Feast of Unity.

All senses are a unity from the viewpoint of reality; from the standpoint of form, they are separate from each other. When one sense is flooded by absorption, all the others follow. When a fly flies it moves its wings, head, legs, and eyes separately; when it is immersed in honey, all its faculties are stilled and united and one, and no part of it makes any movement.

The one who is absorbed is no longer present, and so cannot move or make any effort. He stops acting or moving; he is utterly sunk in the water. Any act or word that comes from him is not his, but the water's action. If there is any selfhood left in him that can make him strike out with his arms or move his hands and feet in the water, or if he is still conscious enough of his own identity to claim, for example, "I am drowning," neither of these states can be called absorption.

A lion was chasing after a deer, and the deer fled from the lion in terror. At first there were two separate beings: the lion and the deer. But when the lion caught up with the deer, and the deer, annihilated beneath the weight of the lion and the furious power of its claws, collapsed in unconsciousness before it, then, at that moment, the lion's being remained alone; the being of the deer was rubbed out.

Both

 "The Beloved is so sweet, so sweet," they repeat;
I show them the scars where His polo-stick thrashed me.
"The Beloved is terrible, a maniac," they wail;
I show them my eyes, melting in His tender passion.

I do not speak these words, Love speaks them
This subject is something I know nothing about.
You can only tell this story if you are a thousand years old.
What can I know? I am a child of the present.
Yet the child I am is a parasite on the Eternal One
And my union with Him ages me centuries.

If you have the serenity to endure a thousand ordeals, and the clear sight to see the new truths and possibilities being born out of blood, and if you go on despite everything that happens, believing in your heart, "The saints and lovers of God have always spoken of patience, patience, and more patience; let me be patient so that what came to them can come to me also"—if you can live like this in continual surrender to God, continually keeping the heart open even in what seems like disaster, then, I swear to you: you *will* reach the Treasure, and in a way and with a power and splendor you could never have imagined. Believe, be patient, endure through all things, and the Door of the Treasury will open and the voice of the King will say, "Enter, my Servant, see and know and be my wonders!" Nothing is more certain than this.

Hear from the heart wordless mysteries! Understand what
    cannot be understood!
In man's stone-dark heart there burns a fire
That burns all veils to their root and foundation.
When the veils are burned away, the heart will understand
    completely
Ancient Love will unfold ever-fresh forms
In the heart of the Spirit, in the core of the heart.

Give me ecstasy, give me naked wonder, O my Creator!
Give birth to the Beloved in me, and let this Lover die!
Let a thousand wrangling desires become one Love!
This ring of desire I wear is the seal of Solomon
I know I have it only on loan, so I never take it off.
The years of repentance are over, a new year has come
That shatters and destroys a thousand regrets a day!
If you never knew this vertigo, this mad Spring will make you
    totter!
O Love, You are the universal soul, crown, and jail all at once;
At once the Prophet's call and our lack of belief.
Love, You have created us with thirsty hearts,
You have bound us to the Source of Splendor.
For You my thorns have blossomed, my atoms embraced
    the worlds.
Contemplating in my leaping atoms the universe
Makes my days stagger and sob with wonder!
Look, the wine is in the green grape, existence in nothingness!
Joseph, I beg you, see in your pit the crown and the kingdom!
A thorn that has not blossomed cannot illumine the field;
How can a being made of water and clay find life
If Divine Breath does not Itself kindle it?
Clap your hands, clap your hands again, and know each sound
Has its origin in the Wine's own self-surrender!
Be silent! Spring is here! The rose is dancing with its thorn.
Beauties have come from the Invisible to call you home.

FOURTH MOVEMENT

On the Path—
Ordeal and Revelation

Love Is the Master

Love is the One who masters all things;
I am mastered totally by Love.
By my passion of love for Love
I have been ground sweet as sugar.
O furious Wind, I am only a straw before you;
How could I know where I will be blown next?
Whoever claims to have made a pact with Destiny
Reveals himself a liar and a fool;
What is any of us but a straw in a storm?
How could anyone make a pact with a hurricane?
God is working everywhere his massive Resurrection;
How can we pretend to act on our own?
In the hand of Love I am like a cat in a sack;
Sometimes Love hoists me into the air
Sometimes Love flings me to the ground.
Love swings me round and round His head;
I have no peace, in this world or any other.
The Lovers of God have fallen in a furious river;
They have surrendered themselves to Love's commands.
Like millwheels they turn, day and night, day and night,
Constantly turning and turning, and crying out.

The moment I saw the Face of my Unique Beloved
I saw my heart in infinite heartache.

Pain the Midwife

Do not run toward pain, but do not run from it either. Pain is your guide. Pain is what guides a person in every serious undertaking. Unless an aching longing and passion arises in someone to get or achieve something, he will never get or achieve it. This is true whatever he may want—whether he wants to be successful in this world or to be saved in the next, or whether he wants to be a king or a powerful banker, a scientist or an astronomer.

Mary only made for the Tree of Blessing when she started to feel the pangs of childbirth. As the Koran tells us, "And birth pangs seized her by the trunk of the palm tree." The pangs that were rending her brought her to the tree, and the tree which had withered became rich with fruit.

This body is like Mary. Every one of us has a Jesus within him, waiting to be born. If pain appears to be our midwife, our divine child will be born. If not, our inner Jesus will return to the Origin by the same secret way he came, and we will be deprived of his mystic joy and splendor. See to the healing of your soul while your Jesus is still here; if he goes back to heaven, all your hope will go with him.

The Only Certain Refuge

Really to experience the day of Resurrection
You have to die first, for "resurrection" means
"Making the dead come back to life."
The whole world is racing in the wrong direction
For everyone is terrified of non-existence
That is, in reality, the only certain refuge.
How should we try to win real awareness?
By renouncing all knowing.
How should we look for salvation?
By giving up our personal salvation.
How should we search for real existence?
By giving up our existence.
How should we search for the fruit of the spirit?
By not always greedily stretching out our hands.

Step by Step

Love, the new moon, grows slowly, stage by stage;
We should progress like that, deliberately, with patience.
I hear the new moon whispering, "Impatient fool!"
It is only step by step you climb to the roof.
Be a seasoned cook, let the pot boil little by little;
A stew cooked in mad haste tastes terrible.
God could have created the universe in a second
Just by issuing the simple order "Be!"
Why, then, did He prolong Creation over six days,
Each one of which equaled a thousand years?
Why does the formation of a child need nine months?
Gradual action is characteristic of the King.
Why did the creation of Adam take forty days?
God perfected his clay by slow, perfect degrees.
Not like you, crazy one, rushing everything always.

For His Lovers, He alone is their joy and grief,
He alone their wages and reward for their service.
If they look to anyone other than the King
Theirs isn't love at all, only an empty passion.
What is Love? That flame which, when it arises,
Consumes everything that is not Him.

The Master of the Work

The grapes of my body can only become wine
After the winemaker tramples me.
I surrender my spirit like grapes to his trampling
So my inmost heart can blaze and dance with joy.
Although the grapes go on weeping blood and sobbing,
"I cannot bear any more anguish, any more cruelty!"
The trampler stuffs cotton in his ears: "I am not
    working in ignorance.
You can deny me if you want, you have every excuse,
But it is I who am the Master of this Work.
And when through my Passion you reach Perfection,
You will never be done praising my name."

Don't Say Yes or No

The fire of hell is just an atom of God's wrath
Just a whip He wields to menace the evil.
Yes, God's wrath is fiery, all-powerful, all-devouring,
But the freshness of His mercy transcends it.
This is an unconditional, unqualified, spiritual priority.
Have you seen beyond duality what is before and behind?
How could a clay bird soar into the heaven of Vision?
The highest place it can soar to is still only air,
For its origin remains sensuality and desire.
Stay, then, astounded and bewildered; don't say yes or no.
Then Mercy can stretch out Its hands to help you.
How could you begin to understand His miracles?
If you said yes glibly you would be lying,
and if you say no, that "no" will behead you
And force severity to slam shut your soul's window.
So stay in bewilderment, in wonder, so God's succor
Can run to you from every side and direction.
When you are really bewildered, maddened and annihilated,
Then your whole being prays, without words, "Guide me!"
The wrath of God is terrible, more terrible than anything,
But once you have begun to tremble, it starts to soften.
Anger is aimed at the denier; when you have become humble
You will come to know it as gentleness, as mercy.

If You Want to See the King

What is the mirror of Being? Not-Being.
Choose Not-Being, if you want to see the King.
Being can only be seen in Not-Being;
The Millionaire shows his lavishness to the beggar.
Bread's clear mirror is the hungry man;
What burns is the mirror of what makes fire.
Non-Being and its defects, wherever they arise,
Are mirrors that reveal the shining of all skills.
If a robe came already sown and cut
How could a tailor show his art?
Tree trunks should be left rough-hewn
So the carpenter can fashion what he needs;
A doctor who mends broken bones
Attends the patient whose leg is broken—
How could the excellence of his skill be shown
Without a weakened, half-crippled man?
How could the splendor of alchemy flash out
If copper's worthlessness and shady character
Were not everywhere known and seen?
Defects are mirrors of the attribute of Perfection;
Our sad condition a mirror of Power and Glory.
Every contrary is made evident by its contrary:
Vinegar's sourness reveals the sweetness of honey.
Whoever has seen and recognized his own defects
Has taken a great stride already toward Perfection.
Vain fool! There is no soul-sickness more harmful
Than pretension to perfection.
Your eyes and heart will have to weep blood
For this vanity to be rooted out.
The great fault of Iblis was to imagine
"I am greater than Adam!"
And this illness lives in each human soul
However humble you imagine you are.

Its only the surface of the water that's clear
There's mud in the stream, you'll discover;
And when the Demon troubles you to test you
The water will once again become mud-colored.
There is dung littering your stream-bed, my friend,
However pure the stream may appear.

Never feel secure from God's power of deception
However many marvelous good fortunes you live through.
If you think you are certain, rub your eyes.
The deception of God is so subtle and ingenious
That your spirit, even if only of this world,
Can believe itself celestial and immortal.
Continue on that path, and destruction is sure.

For Lovers, Hell Is a Garden

On the Last Day, Lovers will say
    to the Angel of Resurrection:
"Isn't hell on the way for everyone?
Don't the faithful as well as unfaithful
Have to go through its terror?
Yet on the path we have traveled until now
We haven't seen either smoke or fire—
Everywhere is Paradise, the Courtyard of Security;
Where then is Hell's horrible passage?"
The Angel of Resurrection will smile and say:
"Remember the green garden you passed on the way?
That was hell, that was the Place of Punishment.
Only for you it became a garden, an orchard of green trees.
Because you have labored
To transform the hell of lust in yourself
And the pride that invites annihilation—
Because you have sweated to make both of these
    transparent to love,
And have exhausted their fire out of love for God,
The fire of your sensual passions
Has become the green force of holiness
And the Light of the True Path.
Your fire of anger has been transformed into patience,
The shadows of ignorance in you have become awareness,
The fire of greed in you has become sacrifice,
The malice that in you was thorns has become roses.
And because you have already extinguished
All these fires which were in you,
And made the fire of your carnal soul like a garden
And sowed in it the seed of fidelity
While the nightingales of the remembrance

And the glorification of God
Sang sweetly in the hedge by the stream—
Since you have answered the call of God
And brought water to the hell of your soul—
Our hell has become for you a green garden
Running with roses and clear laughing springs."

You Cannot Come In until You've Been Cooked

A man came and knocked at the door of his Friend. "Who are you?" asked the Friend. The man said, "It is I." The friend replied, "You cannot come in. There is no room for the 'raw' at my feast, only the fire of absence and separation can cook you and burn you free from vanity. Since your false self has not abandoned you, it must be burned away in fire."

Miserable, the man went away from his Friend's door and for one year suffered his Friend's absence. His heart burned until it was cooked. Then he went again to the house of his Friend.

Again, timidly, fearfully, he knocked at the door. His Friend shouted, "Who is knocking?"

The man replied, "O Beloved, it is You who are at the door!"

"Since it is I," said the Friend, "Come in! In this house there is no room for two 'I's.'"

I groan and my groans ravish Him;
He desires the groaning of the two worlds.
How could I not groan at his deception—
I am not in His drunkards' circle.
How could I not complain, like the night without His day,
Without the Grace of His Gaze that illumines the day?
His harshness is sugar to my soul
I am in love with my pain and suffering
So I can delight my matchless King
I turn grief's dust into collyrium for my eyes
So their two seas can fill with pearls.
Tears that His creatures weep for Him are pearls—
Never say with fools that they are only tears.
I seem to be complaining of the Soul of souls
But really I am only telling my story.
My heart says, "I am tormented by Him,"
But I laugh at its absurd claim.
Do me justice, O Glory of the Just,
You are the Throne, I am just your door's threshold.
Yet where really are "throne" or "threshold"?
In Your district, where are "us" and "I,"
O You whose soul soars above "us" and "I,"
Who permeates with subtle spirit both man and woman?
When man and woman become one, You are that One;
When unities are annihilated, You are that Unity.
You have created this "I" and "Us"
To play the game of adoration with Yourself;
All the "I"s and "You"s will become one single soul
And in the end melt into the Beloved.
All these things are true. Come, Lord, You who orders all things,
Who is beyond all appeal and all description!

This body can only see You in its carnal way;
It has to imagine Your "sadness," Your "laughter."
But how could the heart imprisoned in such fantasies
Ever be worthy of even glimpsing You?
Anyone imprisoned by "sadness" or "laughter"
Is only living off borrowed things.
In the always-green and boundless Garden of Love
There are many other fruits than grief or joy.
My awareness is not bound to imagination or illusion
There is another state of being which is rare as You.

Surrender to the Divine Will

Learn to surrender to the Divine Will
So you will understand quickly
And have a mind fragrant with love of God
When disaster falls on you suddenly.
While others whiten with terror
In the hour of gain or loss,
Laugh like the rose, for the rose—
Even if you tear petal after petal from it—
Never stops laughing and never grows cast down.
"Why," says the rose, "should a thorn sadden me,
When I grew this laugh because of a thorn?"
A man asked, "What is Sufism?" The sheikh replied,
"To feel joy in the heart when anguish comes."
Think of His punishment as like the eagle
That whisked away the Prophet's sandal
To save him from the black snake in it.
God says, "Never despair
At losing what leaves you."
If a wolf comes and destroys your sheep
This misery averts worse misery,
This loss far more terrible loss.

The Man Who Wanted a Tattoo of a Lion

It was the custom in Qazwin for the men to have symbols tattooed on their bodies. A coward went to a tattoo artist and said, "Now please tattoo a lion on my back." As soon as he felt the first prick of the needles he shouted, "What part of the lion are you doing now?" The tattooist replied, "The tail." "Forget the tail; do another part!" The tattooist started on another part of the lion. The man again began to yell and demand that he begin again somewhere else. Wherever the tattooist put his needles, the client screamed. Eventually, the tattooist became so angry that he flung his needles and colors on the floor and refused to go any further.

The King read a letter three times, and did not send an answer. The person who had written it wrote back and complained, "I have petitioned Your Majesty three times now. Please, at least tell me if my petition has been accepted or rejected."

The King wrote on the back of the letter, "Do you not understand that to refuse to answer is itself an answer, and that the answer to a fool is silence?"

What I long for, you know would kill me;
What I think will kill me, you know will heal me.
Loving you, I enter a darkness where I can't see anything.
"You do not need to; I am guiding you by the hand."

The Price

If you want to learn sodomy from sodomites, or prostitution from prostitutes, you cannot learn anything without putting up with a hundred difficulties, beatings, disappointments. How else can you learn and get what you want? How, then, if what you want is Eternal Life, which is the station of the prophets and saints, do you expect to obtain it without suffering or ordeal? How could that be possible?

Imagine someone in love with a man or a woman. Won't that man do everything he can—fawn, flatter, grovel, write plaintive letters, sacrifice time and effort and money, day in and day out—to try and slake the thirst of his passion? Is the love of God less than this? If you could spend on God half the intensity that you spend on yourself, or on your work, or on your hunger for status and possessions, or on your amorous pursuits—then, God knows, God would have no choice but to reveal Himself into you and give you what nothing in the world can give: wisdom, gnosis, and peace.

The Sufi and the Judge

The Sufi said: "God—whose help we implore!
  has the power
To make all our different kinds of business free of loss.
He who transforms the fire of Nimrod into a rose garden
Is fully capable of de-fanging the world's fire.
He who makes roses bloom in a thicket of thorns is also
Capable of transforming every winter into spring.
He who makes a cypress soar tall and wild
Can, if He wants, transmute all grief into ecstasy,
He by whom Non-Being is transfigured into Being—
Would He lose anything if He kept Being always alive?
He gives to the body a soul to make it live—
What would He lose if He didn't make it die?
What would it matter if the King of Magnanimity
Gave His servant what he wanted, without painful travail,
And banished from His frail creations the lures of the flesh
And all the temptations of the Dark One that lie in ambush?"

The Judge replied: "If God did not institute fierce orders,
If there existed neither good nor evil, stones nor pearls,
If the false self did not exist, nor Satan, nor the passions,
And if there were no bitter blows, or battles, or wars,
Then by what title, you idiot, could the King call His servants?
How could he say, 'O patient man! O long-suffering man!'?
How could he say, 'O brave man!' or 'O wise man!'?
Without a devil to test them, how could there be forged
Patient, sincere, forgiving, and generous human beings?
The greatest hero and a male prostitute would rank the same;
Wisdom and awareness would be destroyed and utterly laid waste,
For both of them exist to discriminate between the Real and Unreal,
Between good and evil, between the right and the wrong path;

When all paths are the right one, they're no longer needed.
Do you really think it just that the two worlds should be ruined
So you can keep your shop of shady longings always open?
The cruelty of fate and every affliction that exists
Are less agonizing than being far from God or forgetting him.
Other agonies pass, but forgetfulness remains.
Only that human being who brings at all moments to God
His consciously-awakened spirit can ever possess joy."

The Truth Is within You

Jesus laughed often; John often wept. John said to Jesus, "You must think you are completely safe from all occult and subtle attacks to be able to laugh so much." Jesus laughed and replied, "You must have become very forgetful of God's graces and tendernesses to weep so much."

One of God's lovers was also present at this exchange. He prayed to God and asked Him, "Which of these two is closer to You? Which has the higher rank?" God answered, "The one who has the higher opinion of me."

One of the meanings you can extract from this story is that it is essential to make as rich and beautiful and comprehensive as possible whatever inner image you may have of God; for God comes to you in whatever image you have been able to form of Him. The wiser and broader and more gorgeous the image, the more the grace and power can flow down from the Throne into your heart. God is saying through this story to all of us: "I am where My servant thinks of Me. Every servant has an image of Me; whatever image my servant forms of Me, there I will be. I am the servant of My servant's image of Me. Be careful then, My servants, and purify, attune, and expand your thoughts about Me, for they are My House."

So find out at each moment whether weeping, laughing, fasting or praying, solitude or service, are more profitable to you. Your needs will be constantly changing, so you will have to remain constantly honest and alert. Whichever state brings you more completely onto the Path—more completely and more directly—choose that one, even if it contradicts what you were doing before. Always ask your own heart, however wise the advice a friend or counselor might give you. The truth is within you; compare it with the advice of the wise ones, and where it is in harmony with your truth, follow it.

Wisdom Is Graced to the Weak in Marvelous Ways

What God in His mercy has taught the bees
He has not graced the lion or wild ass;
The bee knows how to make a house of liquid sugar.
It is God who opened to him this Way of Knowledge.
What God in His mercy has taught the silkworm
The elephant himself cannot understand or repeat.
Think of Adam, created from a handful of earth;
Through Grace, he came to begin to know God.
His knowledge radiated light to all seven heavens
And shattered the reputation and pride of angels.
Everyone who is a slave to external sense
Has a muzzle placed on his mouth
So he cannot drink the milk of Truth;
Yet God has dropped into the blood-drop of the heart
A jewel he has denied the seas and skies.
How long will you be obsessed with forms?
How long will your souls doze in externals?
All the lions' heads were bowed
When God blessed the dog of the Companions—
What did his manginess and ugliness matter
When his spirit was plunged in a Sea of Splendor?

The Fur Coat, God, and the Fisherman

There was a teacher who was so poor that in winter he wore only one threadbare cotton robe. A river in spate carried a bear down from the mountains, its head hidden in the swirling water. The children the man was teaching saw the back of the bear and shouted: "Teacher look over there! There's a fur coat in the water! You are always cold, jump in and grab it!"

The teacher jumped in to seize the coat, and the bear, furious, sank his claws into him. The teacher was trapped.

"Teacher!" the boys shouted, "Grab the coat, or if you can't, let it go!" "I am letting the coat go," moaned the teacher, "but it isn't letting *me* go. What can I do?"

How could God's fervor ever let you go? Thank God day and night that we are in His hands and not in ours. How easily we would give up and turn away from Him, if He didn't always hold us to Him in a passion of ownership.

God is like a mother with a child, breastfeeding it to begin with, then weaning it on stronger food, bringing us all through various stages to vision and gnosis. Here in the world we are like children, compared to what we could be in the other world; God does not leave us here but works on us so that, in the end, we realize this world is like childhood, a stage and no more.

You've seen fishermen fishing: they never drag out their fish at once. When the hook has pierced the fish's throat, a fisherman will draw it out little by little, so the fish loses blood and becomes weaker; then he'll tighten it again, then relax it, until the fish is exhausted and waiting to die. When the hook of Love falls into a man's throat, God reels him in gradually so all those twisted faculties and bad blood in him can drain out, little by little.

"How many hooks He has threaded my throat with?"
Gasped the fish, as he struggled and died.
O Fisherman, I bless You, though You killed and ate me!
My passion was always to be alive in You.

Your Stumbling Was a Sign

Don't look at your peacock feathers, look at your feet
So no Evil Eye can ever find you to destroy you.
Before the gaze of evil beings, even a mountain can slip.
Read and take to heart the Koran's words:
    "They disconcert you."
Because of the Evil Eye, Mohammed, who was like a mountain,
Slipped in the middle of the road although there was no mud.
He was astonished and exclaimed: "Why did I slip just now?
What just happened must have a deeper meaning."
Later the verse of the Koran came to him and instructed him
That what had happened sprang from his opponent's hostility.
God said to him: "If it had been anyone but you,
Their Evil Eye would have annihilated him, believe me.
He would have fallen into the abyss of destruction.
But protection streamed from Me and your stumbling was
Only a warning and a sign." So attend to the warnings
That will come, gaze on the Prophet who was a mountain,
Do not expose what you are and have to destruction.
Remember how frail you are, who are less than a straw.

Hard Advice

When the thought "I have done something wrong" enters your mind and you start to reproach yourself, saying, "Why do I do such things?" take this as a sign that God loves you and is looking after you. "Love goes on so long as reproof goes on." Isn't it our friends we bother to reprove? You don't reprove a stranger.

If you perceive a fault in your brother or sister, realize that the fault you see is in yourself. Get rid of that fault in yourself, for what distresses you in the other person is in you.

An elephant was led to a well to drink. He saw himself in the water and reared. He thought he was rearing away from another elephant, and did not realize that in fact he was rearing away from himself.

A man feels no disgust at his own scab or abscess; he will dip his infected hand into the food and lick his fingers without being offended. If he sees, however, a tiny abscess or scratch on someone else's hand, he will avoid that person's food and refuse to eat it. Evil qualities are like scabs and abscesses; when they are in you, you aren't hurt by them, but when you perceive them in someone else you reel in disgust. Dare to turn that disgust not on your neighbor but on your own false self, and, slowly, you will come to know Him in you.

Every time you really look at your false self, you die. After thousands of repeated deaths, you begin to realize what in you lives forever, lives beyond all schemes and fantasies. What you have been searching for all your life will start to appear. Rub and go on rubbing a filthy mirror and however filthy it is to start with, eventually the pure glass will begin to be revealed, and shine.

Things Are Made Clear by Their Opposites

Those who love gold and pearls and rubies look at the reverse of a mirror; those who love the mirror do not look at the pearls and gold. They are always looking at the mirror itself, and they love the mirror for its own sake. Because what they see in the mirror is beautiful, they never grow tired of it. But the person whose face is disfigured by greed and vice sees only faults when he looks directly into the mirror—that is why he so anxiously turns it over and studies the jewels on its back.

In a similar way, God mixes animality and humanity together, so both could be made manifest. "Things are made clear by their opposites." How can you make anything known without its opposite?

God Himself had no opposite. This is why He says: "I was a hidden treasure and wanted to be known." He created this world of darkness so His Light might be known in miraculous and brilliant contrast. He brought forth out of His Being the being of the saints and lovers and mystics and prophets, and said to them: "Go out into My Creation radiant with My Attributes." Holy beings are the theater of the Light of God, and by them real friends can be discerned from secret enemies, real brothers told apart from hostile strangers, the sincere from the hypocrite, true lovers with the searmarks of Love's Fire all over them from those who have hastily made up with ash or charcoal.

As to Reality: Reality has no opposite and cannot have, for All is One; but when Reality manifests in form, then opposites are made obvious. Pharaoh's vanity contrasts with the humility of Moses and deepens our awe at Moses' greatness; Nimrod's hysteria is the darkness against which Abraham's nobility shines calmly; Abu Jahl is the night against which the full moon of Mohammed radiates universal splendor and wisdom. Through the saints and true mystics and prophets, the opposite of God and the Divine Way is disclosed; although, in the final sense, God cannot have any opposite.

Evil has terrifying power in this world of shadows, but that power shrinks when you become aware that evil cannot but serve the brilliance of God's Light even as it tries by every means to annihilate it. Against its brutal and horrifying darkness, the calm stars of Vision, Devotion, and Gnosis shine with deathless clarity, now and forever, the more fervently for the blackness they are set against.

O Happy Sickness

The Prophet visited one of his companions who had fallen sick. Overjoyed to see the Prophet at his bedside, the sick man blessed the illness that made such a holy visit possible, and celebrated the mystery of suffering:

> "O happy sickness, suffering, and fever!
> O blessed torment and insomnia!
> See how in my old age
> God, in his great goodness
> Has graced me such an illness!
> He gave me this piercing pain in my back
> So I should spring out of my sleep at night
> And not doze away like a buffalo.
> God in His mercy has sent me this anguish
> And because of it the mercy of kings has awoken
> And the threats of hell have been rubbled to nothing."

Suffering is a treasure, for it conceals mercies;
The almond becomes fresh when you peel off the rind.
O my brother, staying in a cold dark place
And bearing patiently the grief, weakness, and pain
Is the Source of Life and the cup of Abandon!
The heights are found only in the depths of abasement;
Spring is hidden in autumn, and autumn pregnant with spring.
Flee neither; be the friend of Grief, accept desolation,
Hunt for the life that springs from the death of yourself.

The Fire of the King will descend to roast you
Run like a coward and you'll always stay unripe.
Open your entire being to Its flames, and you'll become
Cooked completely, like sweet-smelling, fresh-baked bread.
You will be the King and Bride at the table.

On Good and Evil

If anyone could be Pure Love and Pure Knowledge, without any stain of ignorance anywhere—that person would immediately be burned up in the Fire and cease to exist at all. So ignorance is in some ways "desirable," because without it we would stop existing; and knowledge and love too are "desirable," because they lead to proximity and intimacy. Ignorance and knowledge seem to be opposites; they are in fact secret allies.

The same is true of night and day. Night is not the enemy or opposite of day, but its ally. If night lasted forever, no work would ever get accomplished; if day went on and on without any rest or interruption, everyone would go insane and be able to do nothing. So people rest at night, refresh and reinvigorate themselves so that they can spend their renewed powers by day.

To the one Love has instructed, things that seem opposite reveal their secret affinity and relation. Show me the evil in this universe in which no good at all is contained, or the good in which there is not the slightest touch of evil!

I heard once about a man who was consumed with the desire to murder someone, but went to a prostitute and worked off his anger in lust. Lust is an evil; insofar as indulging it prevented the man from murder, it is a kind of good. So evil and good cannot be separated. Show me good without evil, so I can agree that there is a God of Good and a God of Evil. You cannot—because good does not exist apart from evil. Knowing this does not bring any acceptance of evil—evil remains evil, to be fought and defeated. But knowing this lessens fear.

God Wills Both Good and Evil

God wills both good and evil, but only welcomes and blesses the good. God never blesses evil, otherwise He would not have ordered the good. God is like a teacher who wants to teach; what can he teach if the pupil is not ignorant? To desire something is also to desire what makes it possible. The teacher does not, however, bless the pupil's ignorance, otherwise he would not teach him. Doesn't a doctor need people to be ill for him to be able to heal them? Yet he doesn't bless the fact that people are ill, otherwise he wouldn't attend them with such care. A baker requires people to be hungry, otherwise how would he sell his bread and support his family? But he doesn't bless hunger and want it to continue, otherwise why would he sell bread at all?

Soldiers want their king to have an enemy—otherwise how will they ever prove their courage and their love for him? They do not in any way bless their king's enemy—why then would they fight? In a similar way, a man can come to desire temptations because he knows God loves and blesses the being who is grateful, obedient, and righteous in the glare of provocation, and that this blessing is not possible without the existence of temptation. (To desire something, as I have said, is to desire what makes it possible.) But he does not in any way bless these assaults; he fights with his whole heart and mind to repel them. From these analogies—however inadequate they are—I think you can see how in one way God does will evil and how in another way He does not.

There are some who claim: "God does not will evil in any way at all." This is not true; how could God will anything without willing those things which make it possible? Essential to His Plan and Order is man's stubborn, often ignorant, and often reckless soul which inherently, it seems, longs for evil and flees from good. Are you going to tell me that God did not will what makes the disposition of such a soul possible—all the evils and temptations of this world? If God had not willed these, He would not have willed the soul; and if He had not willed the soul, He would not have issued any of the commands and prohibitions that apply to the soul's growth and destiny. If, however, God had in any way blessed these evils, or in any way not wanted to mitigate their horror, He would not have issued such stern orders or made the soul subject to such warnings and holy rigor.

God wants us to choose the Diamond of Love, and he wants that choice to transfigure us by stages into perfected ecstatic beings. What would such a choice be worth if beside the diamond there weren't a thousand glittering things that could distract and swerve us from it? The choice of the Diamond has to come from our full being. We must know what it costs and be prepared to pay its extreme price freely for the full gift of its shining to be given to us. This is His Law: nothing can or will change it. And because it is His Law there is a mystery of Love in it that no one can wholly describe or explain.

The Driver's Grace

Jesus was wandering in the desert when a thunderstorm broke. He went to take shelter in the corner of a jackal's cave. A voice spoke to him: "Get out of the cave immediately; the jackal's pups can't sleep because you are here." Jesus cried out in anguish, "Lord, the jackal's pups have shelter, but the Son of Mary has nowhere to lay his head!"

The jackal may have a home, a warm place out of the rain, a shelter for his wife and children. But he does not have a Beloved like Jesus' to drive him out of his home. Blessed is the one who has such a One driving him out continually from his safe places; the magnanimity of such a Driver, the grace of the robe of honor that continual exile alone confers—to know these and experience them is more precious than millions of worlds and heavens, thrones and footstools.

Whatever Instrument He Makes of Me

Do not, like an idiot, be at mercy of the spear
But of the King whose hand brandishes it.
Crying out to the spear and sword are absurd;
They are just slaves in the Noble One's hands.
Whatever instrument He makes of me, I am.
If He makes of me a cup, I am a cup;
I am a dagger if He makes me a dagger.
If He makes me a fountain, water pours out of me;
Heat dances from me if He makes me a fire.
If He makes me rain, I give birth to rich fields;
If He makes me an arrow, I pierce hearts;
If He makes me a serpent, poison flames from me.
If He makes me a friend, I serve my friends.
He is the Writer; I am the pen in His fingers.
Who am I to obey or disobey?

On Gratitude

What does God do when he loves one of his servants? He afflicts him. If the servant endures with stamina and sincerity, God chooses him. If he is grateful, God elects him. Some people are grateful to God for His anger, and some for His tenderness. Both responses are wise; gratitude is a philosopher's stone that transforms affliction into grace. The perfect human being is the one who can be grateful for fierce treatment, both openly and secretly; such a being is one of the Elect.

A foreigner lived near one of the Companion's messengers in an upstairs room. From his apartment all kinds of dirt and filth, his dirty washing water and his and his children's excrement, flowed down into the Companion's living quarters. The Muslim never complained; he always thanked the foreigner and told his children to do the same. Things went on like this for eight years, until the Companion died. When the foreigner came in to condole with his family, he saw how filthy the apartment was, and where and how the filth arrived there. He realized what had been happening all these years and was mortified and wailed in front of everyone, "Why on earth didn't you tell me what was happening? Why did you always thank me?" The Muslim's family replied, "Our father told us to be grateful in all circumstances, and warned us against ever ceasing to be grateful." The foreigner became a believer.

Be grateful for your life, every detail of it, and your face will come to shine like a sun, and everyone who sees it will be made glad and peaceful. Persist in gratitude, and you will slowly become one with the Sun of Love, and Love will shine through you its all-healing joy. This path of gratitude is not for children; it is the path of tender heroes, of the heroes of tenderness who, whatever happens, keep burning on the altar of their hearts the flame of adoration.

The Wind in the House

Keep the Real always passionately and stubbornly in view and duality will dissolve, burn away like a paper-chain in the fire of Love. Duality, after all, is a characteristic of the branches of a tree; its root is One.

Think of a wind gusting through a house. It flips up the edges of carpets, makes all the rugs in all the rooms rustle and leap. It throws into the air sticks and straws, ruffles a pool and transforms its surface into a coat of shimmering chain mail, gets trees and their branches dancing like acrobats. All of these states appear distinct, appear different, especially to the normal mind that so loves to differentiate and categorize everything. Yet, from the standpoint of the root cause and from the standpoint of essential reality, all of these seemingly distinct states and events are in fact set in motion, caused, and orchestrated by the one omnipresent, invisible, infinitely supple wind.

Meditate on this. Something astonishing will suddenly become clear.

The Two Veils

There are two veils between God and human beings: health and wealth. All other veils are offshoots of these. Someone who is well says, "Where is this God you are always talking about? I don't see Him anywhere." As soon as pain has him in its claws, however, you'll find him begging, "Oh God, help me! Save me! Heal me!" Suddenly, he will be desperate to commune with that very God whose existence he denied when he was well. So you see, health was for him a veil between himself and God, and under his pain and its torments, God was hidden.

The same is true of wealth. You must have seen a thousand times how rich people who have everything they could possibly need spend their time grabbing more and more so that they can gratify themselves. The thought of God never crosses their minds; the exaggerated respect that the world in general pays wealth often convinces the rich that they are wonderful, and this blinds them further. See one of these fools go bankrupt or lose a fortune in a bad business deal or in war, and you'll see his pride suddenly rubbled, and he will begin at last to turn to God.

As the poet says:

> *Drunkenness and empty-handedness drew You to me;*
> *I am the slave of Your drunkenness and poverty.*

Poor Pharaoh! God gave him 400 years of omnipotent luxurious life. What a curse! Such a life in its pride and splendor was the thickest imaginable veil between him and the Presence. Pharaoh didn't have a single day of pain or self-doubt or worry or humiliation, so why should he ever need to remember God? The glory God gave him was in fact a punishment. Blinded by his own petty little sun, Pharaoh never at any time needed to try and find and gaze at the real Sun, whose Light consumes and obliterates all others. God said to him, in effect, "Go on being obsessed with your own fantasies and desires; satisfy them all, if you want. Your curse will be: never to remember me. Goodnight, emperor of the world!"

King Solomon grew exhausted by his long magnificent reign. But Job, the true lover, never grew tired of his pain.

Things Are Made Clear by Their Opposites

Whoever speaks harshly of a Lover in fact speaks well of him. I'll explain: once a Lover has been shown a quality in him that shames him, he rears away from it. He becomes that quality's enemy. So, the one who denigrates that quality is denigrating the enemy of the Lover and actually praising the Lover himself, for he now loathes and rejects that quality, and to avoid the despicable is noble. Things are made clear by their opposites. So a Lover knows that his accuser is not really his enemy, or is his enemy only in his own mind, and by pointing out an imperfection in him—however savagely and with whatever malicious intention—has actually befriended him and helped him deepen his self-knowledge and progress along the Path of Perfection.

I am a smiling garden ringed about by a filthy jagged wall. On that wall there are large, cruel-looking thorns. If you pass by, you will not see the garden; you will see only the wall with all its thorns, filth, and jaggedness, and you will speak harshly of it. Why should I, the garden, be angry with you? Your evil talk only limits you, not me; after all, there is no other way into my rose garden except over the wall! By finding easy fault with the wall—frankly, any fool with eyes would see the same as you—you stay away from my rose garden. So you have only achieved your own isolation and destruction.

The Prophet said, "I laugh as I kill." He has no enemy; when he "kills," he saves. If he "kills" someone (and by this I mean he transforms them by "killing" their dark lower self), all he is doing is saving that one from killing himself in a thousand perverse and deadly ways. So, of course, the Prophet laughs as he kills.

They Continue at Their Prayers

Prayer is not just for the set times of kneeling and bowing; the real challenge of prayer is to prolong that state of absorption always, to keep the heart in a constant blaze of adoration whether you are asleep or awake, writing or reading. In all circumstances and every situation, see that you never wander from God's hand. What is said in the Koran, "They continue at their prayers," should also describe you.

Thus speaking and being silent, sleeping and eating, being angry and then forgiving, is all like the revolving of a waterwheel. A waterwheel turns only from the force of water; it may try to turn on its own, but with no result. The height of ignorance and absurdity is when the waterwheel imagines that it turns by itself.

This turning of the wheel occurs in a confined space, for the circumstances and situations of this material world are narrow. So cry to God and say, "O God, instead of my current way of turning, instead of the present confinement of my journey—grace me another, more vast mystical turning! All needs are fulfilled by You, and Your Generosity and Compassion are universal and all-embracing!" Don't be too proud or too afraid to present your needs to God constantly; never, for one moment, be without remembrance of Him. The remembrance of God is force, power, strength, and endurance; it is feathers and wings to the bird of the Spirit. If you realize perpetual remembrance, and make your life a constant calling-down and invoking of the Presence into everything, that is Light upon Light.

By remembering God constantly, the heart becomes illumined and detachment from the world and its games grows deeper and deeper. There is a bird in you that wants to soar to heaven. It may not be able to reach heaven, but every moment it can rise further from the earth and soar beyond other birds. There is a beautiful box in front of you with musk in it; you can put your hand into the box and although you may not be able to take out the musk, still your hand becomes fragrant, and when you smell it you smile with joy.

Be at Least as Clever as a Dog

You cannot see a sword when it is hidden in its scabbard. If you want to become a Sword of the Faith—a human being who fights for truth and justice, whose life mirrors divine beauty and righteousness—then you must first fight with yourself, and work implacably to refine and ennoble you own character. "Begin with yourself," says the Koran.

Before you can advise others you must have learned how to advise yourself. Say to yourself, as I do, "I have arms, legs, a mouth, and hands just like Mohammed or Bayazid or Al-Hallaj, just like all those saints and prophets and holy beings who have come into the stable ecstasy of the Presence—why did the Presence reveal Itself to them and not to me? Why should I not also come into Its Glory? Why should they be the only ones to pass through the Door? Didn't they begin just as I have?"

And when you let the full outrageous challenge of these words penetrate your dullness—the challenge that Divine Grace is always holding out to everyone who works and suffers enough—then you will start to fight and box with yourself day and night. You will say to yourself, as I do a hundred times a day, "Why are you not accepted? What darkness or dirtiness remains in you that the Presence doesn't show you always Its Face?" It is heroic to confront yourself like this continually, for you will be left, if you persist, no vanity or consolation to hide in. If you persist in this sometimes lacerating heroism, in the anguish of this continual confrontation with your own pettiness, greed, and darkness, then you will become the Sword of God and the Tongue of Truth.

There are ten people outside a house. Nine are invited in; the tenth is left outside. Wouldn't this person lament, "What have I done to be left out? Were my manners awful? Have I done something I am not aware of?" The last thing to do would be to accept exclusion with a corrupt resignation masquerading as humility. The last thing you should say to yourself is: "I cannot enter because it is God's will that I should not. If He had wanted me to go into his House he would have shown me the way and opened the Door." This is rubbish, and amounts to insulting God. When you talk like this to yourself, you become the Sword against God and not the Sword *for* God.

God is too high and majestic to have any "family." He has not given birth and has never been born. No one has ever found the Way to Him except through servanthood. God does not for one moment need you; He is self-sufficing, self-complete, and full. You are the one who needs Him. This is true for everyone—even the greatest of the prophets and saints. So you never have any excuse for saying, "Ah, he or she is more favored by God than I am, more elect, more naturally gifted, more God's child and familiar, more intimately connected." This is pride and evasion hiding themselves behind a mask of humility.

No one has ever attained to friendship with God, to the Presence, except through servanthood. God is always the Only and Absolute King of Gifts; it was God who filled the lap of the sea with pearls, who arrayed the bare thorn in the glory of the rose, who gave life to a handful of dust, all from pure tenderness.

If you heard that there was a billionaire living in a town close to you who delighted in giving away wads of dollar bills and helping everyone who asked him, wouldn't you do everything possible to go and see him? The entire universe with all its million splendors is only one atom of the generosity of God, one small gold coin flung to us from His infinite treasury that at all times lies open to His lovers. Why don't you beg of Him what you need and want? Why don't you trust Him, and trust that you will receive from Him a robe of honor and splendid gifts? You just sit grumpily and lazily, saying, "If He wills, then He will give it to me." And so you do not beg Him for anything, you don't make good any demands on Him. You treat Him as if He were not the All-Merciful and All-Magnificent and All-Lavish One; by not asking God, in fact, you indulge in a subtle form of blasphemy.

A dog is cleverer than you. When a dog is starving, doesn't it come up to you wagging its tail and begging a bit of bread? Are you less than a dog? A dog isn't content to sleep in ashes and moan, "Well, if he wants to, he will give me bread." It accosts you and barks and wags its tail. Why don't you just wag your tail and beg what you want from God? In the presence of such a King of Gifts, begging shamelessly isn't disgraceful, it is natural—a requirement, in fact.

God is closer to you than you can now imagine. Every thought, every idea you have, God is creating in you. He is so close, so near, in fact, that you cannot see Him. This shouldn't surprise you. Every act you perform you perform on the inspiration of some thought or logic; can you see that thought or logic? You see its effect; you do not see its essence.

A man went to the baths. Wherever he walks in the baths he feels heat; fire is with him, and he feels hot through the effects of the fire. While in the baths themselves he doesn't see the fire, but he feels its effects. When he leaves the baths, he sees the fire and realizes that is where all the heat of the baths came from. A human being is a vast bath, heated by Reason and Spirit and Soul. When you leave this bath and go to the Source of Fire, you will see the essence of the Reason, Spirit, and Soul that heated your being. You will realize that your cleverness was engendered by Reason's heat, that all your illusions and fantasies sprang from the Soul, and that your life was the effect of the heat of the Spirit. You will grasp directly the essence of all three powers; out of the bath at last, you will see the Fire that feeds all its different kinds of fertile heat.

Think of someone who has never seen running water. Fling him into a river with his eyes bandaged. Something wet and pliant and infinitely soft will hit against his body, but he won't have any idea what it is. Take the covering off his eyes and he'll see that it was water. First he knew its effects, then its essence was revealed to him.

So beg God, demand what you need and want; you will find you *cannot* ask in vain. Do Our Father and Mother not say to us tenderly in the Koran: "Call upon Me, and I will answer you"?

The Prophets Are Us

Everything visible is visible because of concentration. The breath in hot weather cannot be seen; in cold it can. Cold concentrates it. A prophet's duty is to concentrate and so manifest the splendor of God, and to awaken human beings by speaking and preaching the Divine Truth. It is not the prophet's duty, and cannot be, to bring each being to the stage where he or she is ready to receive God's truth. That is always the work of God alone.

God has essentially two attributes: anger and tenderness. The prophets and saints and holy beings are theaters of both; to those who believe, they are a theater of God's tenderness; to those who do not, they are a theater of God's anger. Those who know and obey and acknowledge the truth see their true selves in the prophet as in a mirror; they hear their own inmost and truest voice come out of them, and they smell their own fragrance as it breaks out from their presence and words. No human being can deny her deepest self. This is why the prophet and saints and holy beings say to the community: "We are you, and you are us; there is never any separation between us."

Such words challenge us. For if we really are the prophets, then what excuse do we have to go on acting like jackals and vipers? If we really are them (which is what they have discovered in the glory of vision and in the abyss of humility), then we must change everything.

Why have the true prophets again and again been reviled, slandered, betrayed, even killed? Because the true prophets reveal to us exactly what we could be, if we only worked and prayed and struggled, humbly and passionately enough. They offer no easy solutions, no false consolations, no flatteries, no fake miracles, no all-purpose panaceas. This we cannot bear, because we cannot bear truth, and so we mock and kill them.

Two things remain to be said: Blessed are they who can listen to the Good News about themselves and die to enact it in this life. And: Everyone is called to be blessed in this way.

Never Lose Hope of God

Never lose hope of God, however terrible and confusing the circumstances you find yourself in. Hope is the head of the road to confidence. If you do not walk along that road, at least guard with all your powers its entryway. Do not go on saying, "I have done twisted things"; choose the truthful way and no twistedness will remain. Truth is like Moses' rod, and all twisted thoughts and actions are like the tricks of Pharaoh's magicians; when Truth arrives, it swallows up all those games. If you have done evil, it is to yourself that you have done it; nothing in that evil could ever touch or darken the Eternal Face of God. Just commit yourself unwaveringly to truth and, slowly, all your twistedness will be burned away.

Hope is the source and spring of all the alchemies of transformation, the greatest treasure of the heart and mind, the philosopher's stone that transmutes agony and tragedy into new life. Never abandon hope, or you abandon your closest and most helpful guide, the Friend who will be at the door of Paradise smiling as he lets you in.

Be Always Humble

If everything was as it appeared to be, why then would the Prophet, gifted as He was with the most penetrating and illumined inner vision, have repeatedly cried out: "Lord, show me things as they are. You make a thing appear beautiful and in reality it is hideous; You make a thing appear hideous and, in fact, it is instinct with the greatest beauty. Show us then, O Lord, everything just as it really is, so we do not fall into Your traps and wander lost in darkness."

You may have excellent and refined judgment but, however good it may be, it is unlikely to be better than the Prophet's. He used to speak in this way again and again. So, for His sake and yours, do not put your trust in every idea and concept that occurs to you. Be always humble, in awe, and fearful before God.

Never Despair

In the Koran, God says:

> "O Prophet, tell the prisoners in your power
> If God knows of any good hidden in your hearts
> He will give you in return
> More, far more, than has been taken from you.
> And he will forgive you,
> For God is all-forgiving, all-compassionate."

This verse was revealed in the following situation: Mohammed (may God bless him and give him peace) had defeated the unbelievers, killing many and taking many prisoners and chaining them hand and foot. His uncle Abbas was among them. The prisoners wept and howled all night, and in their humiliation they had given up hope. They expected only death. The Prophet looked at them and laughed.

The prisoners murmured bitterly among themselves, "So you see—the Prophet is just like anyone else. All his claims to be different are nonsense. He is just like any other passion-driven man: he gloats over and mocks his enemies when he has beaten them."

The Prophet saw what was in their hearts. "What you are saying is not at all true. It is not in me to laugh at my enemies because I have beaten them, or because I see them grieving. Do you want to know why I am laughing? With my inner eye, I see something extraordinary: I am dragging a whole people—against their will—out of their fiery furnace and smoky hell into Paradise and the fragrance of the Eternal Rose Garden, and all they are doing is howling and lamenting, 'Why are you dragging us out of the pit of destruction into the safety of the rose garden?' Naturally, laughter overcomes me.

"Because you haven't yet been given the understanding to see and know what I'm telling you, God orders me to say this: 'First you collected together your armies, trusting in your strength and power, and boasted among yourselves, "This is what we are going to do: we are going to thrash and subjugate the Muslims easily." You did not reckon with the All-Powerful One when you vaunted your own power; you did not think or even know of the One whose force incomprehensibly outstrips yours. So, of course, everything you planned turned out contrary to your plans. Even your fear now is a continuation of your old arrogance; you wallow in despair and still do not see the One who has all power over you. See My Power now, see My Strength, know yourselves slaves of My Will, so that I may make all things gentler for you. You shake in terror—but even in this terror, never despair of Me; My Power is fully capable of releasing you from the prison of any fear and of making you safe and strong. If I can produce a black bull out of a white one, I can also produce a white one out of a black. Did I not make the day go into the night and the night go into the day? Did I not bring out the living from the dead, and the dead from the living? You are prisoners now, yes, but never despair of Me, of My Presence. Let Me take each of you by the hand, for:

> Let no human being ever despair
> Of being consoled by God
> Except those who do not believe.'"

God Does It All

> "When the help of God arrives, and victory with it, and you witness men entering God's religion in crowds, then proclaim the praise of Your Lord, and ask His forgiveness: for He always turns again to men."

Traditional commentators expound on this *sura* in the following way: "Mohammed, may God bless him and give him peace, had the ambition to make the whole world Muslim and bring everyone into the Path of the One. When he saw death coming he cried out in anguish, 'Alas! I did not live to accomplish my desire to call all men to God!' God answered, 'Do not grieve. At the very moment you die, I, by My Grace, will convert cities and provinces to the Faith that you would have had to conquer in battle. You will receive a Sign: when you are dying you will see men entering in great crowds clamoring to become Muslims. When this Sign comes, know that you will soon die. Then give praise and ask for forgiveness.'"

There is an esoteric interpretation of this that is more profound. People imagine that they will purify themselves of their darkness by work and striving. When they have struggled passionately and exhausted all their powers, they fall into despair. Then God says to them, "Did you really imagine that everything would happen through your power? The Law I have laid down is this: whatever you have, spend it in My Way. Then My Grace will intervene. My command is: set out on My Road, just as you are, with your weak hands and weak feet. I know very well that with such feeble feet you will never finish the journey; in fact, if you took a hundred thousand years, you still, on your own, would not be able to finish even the first stage of this journey. Set out on the Road nevertheless; for when you faint with exhaustion and have no more strength, I Myself, in My loving Providence and Mercy, will carry you. When a child is still being breastfed it is carried in its parents' arms. When it is strong enough to walk, it is set free. Often as you struggled I gave you glimpses of My Magnificence and Grace, and these strengthened you and fed you hope. Now you are destitute and desolate, and have finally given up all hope of accomplishing anything on your own and with your own powers, I will show you the truth of My Love and shower you with graces and tendernesses you never imagined even in the heights of ecstasy. Look, Mohammed, men are coming to you in such thousands! You would not have seen even an atom of this by your own efforts, however immense and heroic.

"Then proclaim the praise of Your Lord and ask for His forgiveness. Ask forgiveness then for all your fantasies and all your vanity. You really believed that your task would be done by your hands and feet; you did not realize that it would all be brought about by Me, and by Me alone. Now you have seen this, ask My forgiveness, 'For He always turns again to men.'"

Just Ask God

A dervish taught his son that whenever he wanted anything he should just ask God for it. If he wept and begged God for what he wanted, God would bring it to him. Years passed. One day, the child was alone in the house and wanted some soup. So he said to God, "I want some soup." Suddenly, from the other world materialized a bowl of soup, and the child ate and drank his fill. When his father and mother came back they said, "Aren't you hungry by now? Don't you want something to eat?" The child said, "I just asked for some soup, thank you. It came, and I ate." His father was deeply moved, "God be forever praised! You have come so far, my son, your reliance on God has become so strong!"

When Mary's mother bore her, she made a vow to dedicate her daughter to the House of God and not to interfere in her upbringing in any way. So she left her in a corner of the temple. There she was found by the high priest Zachariah who demanded to look after her, as did all the other priests. At that time it was customary to settle disputes in the following way: everyone concerned threw a stick on water; the one whose stick floated, won. Zachariah won and Mary was handed over to his care. Every day, Zachariah would bring food to the child, and every day he would always find the exact replica of what he was bringing her in the same corner of the temple. He asked her, "Where do you get the other food?" Mary said, "Whenever I feel hungry I ask God, and whatever I ask God, He sends. His Generosity and Compassion are infinite; whoever relies wholly on Him finds His help never fails!"

What Mary said inspired Zachariah, who started to pray out loud, "O God, since You allow everyone's need, I also have a desire. I long for a son who will be Your Friend; who, without any prompting from me, will live with You and in You." And God brought John the Baptist into being, although his father was weak and hunched-over and his mother was, seemingly, long past childbearing.

All things are in God's hands. To God, no miracle is impossible. God can do anything, God *will* do anything, for anyone who believes and trusts in Him.

The believer is the one who knows that behind all things there is Someone who knows exactly everything he is, thinks, and does, and who sees him completely even though He cannot be seen. The unbeliever is the one who thinks this is all rubbish, a fairytale told to fools by fools. The day will come when God will shake and admonish him; then he will be sad and moan, "I spoke evil and wandered in darkness. Everything was Him, and I denied Him."

If I Sit in My Own Place

I know that God will give me my daily bread. There is no need to run about and waste my energies needlessly. In fact, when I gave up any ideas of money, food, clothes, of satisfying physical desire, then everything began to come to me naturally. When I run after what I think I want, my days are a furnace of distress and anxiety; if I sit in my own place of patience, what I need flows to me, and without any pain. From this I understand that what I want also wants me, is looking for me and attracting me; when it cannot attract me any more to go to it, it has to come to me. There is a great secret in this for anyone who can grasp it.

What I am saying is: busy yourselves with the business of the Other World, and everything in this world will run after you. When I said, "I am sitting in my own place in patience," what I meant by "sitting" is sitting as applied to the business of the world to come. If you sit occupied with the world to come you are in fact running; if you run about for the affairs of this world you are actually staying still and not doing anything real. Didn't the Prophet say: "Make all your concerns one single concern and God will look after all your other concerns"? Say there are ten worries nagging at you; choose the one about the Divine World, and God personally will see to the other nine worries without any need for you to do anything. There is a great secret in this for anyone who can grasp it.

The difference between birds with wings and holy people with the Wings of passionate Love, is that birds with their wings fly in a certain direction, which is always changing, and holy beings with Wings of Love long only to fly away from all directions.

> You are a placeless fire
> All places burn away in,
> A whirlpool of Nowhere
> Drowning me deeper, deeper.

Dancing is not rising to your feet painlessly like a whirl of dust blown about by the wind. Dancing is when you rise above both worlds, tearing your heart to pieces and giving up your soul.

> Dance while you can shatter your own self
> And pluck out the cotton from the wound
>   of self-obsession.
> Ordinary people dance and frolic in the square;
> Men of God dance in their own blood.

O Master of the wineshop, pour me a cup now!
Don't say "tomorrow"; waiting brings despair.
If you have no wine, pour Pharaoh's blood;
The Moses of my soul has come to the meeting
And his wine is the blood of the Enemy.
Lions love hunting: how bloody their jaws and claws are!
It is my blood that gushes all over them.
I don't need the primrose, or the blood of the vine;
I am drunk on negation, not on affirmation.
I am a hawk, I love to catch living prey;
I don't circle like a vulture around corpses.
Vulture, come here quickly! Dare to become a hawk!
Pitch "vulturehood" into the cauldron, become pure.
Then give up even the attributes of the hawk,
Soar higher and transform your essence.
The world isn't dirt, but a cup full of blood
Running over with the blood of lovers and their wounds.
Cock, how many more times will you crow at dawn?
The dimming lamps announce: Morning has come!

What is copper that, when the philosopher's stone arrives,
Its "copperness" should not be annihilated by gold's attribute?
What is a tiny insignificant seed that, when Spring arrives,
It should not be annihilated for a tree to arrive?
All intellects and all sciences are only stars; You are
The Sun of the cosmos that burns all their veils away.
This world is snow and ice, and You are the fiery summer;
No sign of anything remains when the King's Signs flame out!
Who am I—tell me!—that I could exist a moment near You?
Just one of your sidelong glances, My Beloved, destroys me.

In the presence of the Beloved, a Lover recalled his ordeals:
"For You, I suffered all horrors in a long war.
Wealth has gone, and strength, and reputation;
    because of my love
For You, many, many miseries have attacked me.
Not one dawn found me laughing, not one evening calm."
Everything that he had tasted of desolation and despair
The Lover told his Beloved, detail by detail, point by point.
And not from revenge at all: he was only offering
A hundred clear testimonies to the reality of his passion.
The Beloved replied, "Yes, you did suffer all those things.
But open your eyes wide now, and listen very carefully:
You have not accomplished at all what is the root of the root
Of love and fidelity; what you have done is only the branches."
The Lover cried out: "Tell me, then, what is this root?"
He replied: "To die to yourself and to be annihilated."
"You did all the rest," He added, "but still you are not dead."
At once the Lover prostrated himself and gave up his soul.
Like the rose, he gave up his life, laughing and rejoicing,
And this laughter stayed with him, like a gift, for eternity.

Leap Free

In that moment you are drunk on yourself
The friend seems a thorn.
In that moment you leap free of yourself, what use is the friend?
In that moment you are drunk on yourself
You are the prey of a mosquito;
And the moment you leap free of yourself, you go elephant hunting.
In that moment you are drunk on yourself
You lock yourself away in cloud after cloud of grief;
And in that moment you leap free of yourself
The moon catches you and hugs you in its arms.
That moment you are drunk on yourself, the friend abandons you.
That moment you leap free of yourself, the wine of the friend,
In all its brilliance and dazzle, is held out to you.
That moment you are drunk on yourself
You are withered, withered like autumn leaves.
That moment you leap free of yourself
Winter to you appears in the dazzling robes of spring.
All disquiet springs from the search for quiet;
Look for disquiet and you will come suddenly upon a field of quiet.
All illnesses spring from the scavenging for delicacies;
Renounce delicacies, and poison itself will seem delicious to you.
All disappointments spring from your hunting for satisfactions;
If only you could stop, all imaginable joys
Would be rolled like pearls to your feet.
Be passionate for the friend's tyranny, not his tenderness,
So the arrogant beauty in you can become a lover who weeps.
When the king of the feast, Shams-ud-Din, arrives from Tabriz,
God knows you'll be ashamed then of the moon and stars.

Love's Horse Will Carry You Home

The whole world could be choked with thorns
A Lover's heart will stay a rose garden.
The wheel of heaven could wind to a halt
The world of Lovers will go on turning.
Even if every being grew sad, a Lover's soul
Will still stay fresh, vibrant, light.
Are all the candles out? Hand them to a Lover—
A Lover shoots out a hundred thousand fires.
A Lover may be solitary, but he is never alone
For companion he has always the hidden Beloved.
The drunkenness of Lovers comes from the soul,
And Love's companion stays hidden in secret.
Love cannot be deceived by a hundred promises;
It knows how innumerable the ploys of seducers are.
Wherever you find a Lover on a bed of pain
You find the Beloved right by his bedside.
Mount the stallion of Love and do not fear the path—
Love's stallion knows the way exactly.
With one leap, Love's horse will carry you home
However black with obstacles the way may be.
The soul of a real Lover spurns all animal fodder,
Only in the wine of bliss can his soul find peace.
Through the Grace of Shams-ud-Din of Tabriz, you will possess
A heart at once drunk and supremely lucid.

FIFTH MOVEMENT

Fruition

Love is here like the blood in my veins and skin
He has annihilated me and filled me only with Him
His fire has penetrated all the atoms of my body
Of "me" only my name remains; the rest is Him.

In the Eternal Presence you are both Witness
　　and Witnessed—
How you laugh now at all the language of "searching"!
You have lifted up your head between Obliteration
　　and Annihilation—
How you laugh at all the proud games of power!

I look for my heart and find it in your house
I search for my soul and find it in your hair
Whenever I am thirsty, I drink water
I see in it only the image of Your Face.

"I came to take you by the hand
To rob you of your heart and your self
And root you in the Heart and Soul.
At the height of spring I came, O rosebush,
To fold you in my arms and embrace you;
I came to give you, here in this house, My splendor
And to carry you away to heaven, like the prayer of lovers."

I was snow, I melted in your rays
The earth drank me: mist, now, and pure spirit,
I climb back to the Sun.

What is there in the jar that isn't also in the river?
What can you find in the house that is not in the city?
This world is the jar, the Heart the river;
This world is the house, the Heart the city of miracles.

"You are not just yourself, my Friend, you are the sky and the deep
sea. This powerful You is a thousand times bigger than the sea, in
which a thousand 'you's could be drowned."

This morning, Contemplation led me to a garden
Neither outside this world nor within it.
"Garden of miracles!" I asked, "What kind of garden are you?"
It smiled. "One that fears neither winter nor autumn."

May a wind from His Garden breathe you this secret:
It is not only I who am speaking here
But you, too, your own soul, your own heart—
Only for you are we ever apart.

So many other glorious things to be said
The Spirit will say them to you now, not me.
Rather, you yourself will whisper them in your own ear
Neither I—or someone other than I—will say them,
You who are myself!

Grace Is the Door

Cupbearer, pour the wine! Let it flow and keep flowing!
I am sick of swinging between hope and fear.
Shatter thought, I want nothing to do with it!
Tear from my heart all unstable imaginings!
Hack from their chains the shameless joys of passion!
Dance into our assembly, Beloved, unveil Your Face,
Scatter graces with each swirl of Your robe of flame.
Look at these madmen dancing out of themselves for You:
See how they've stripped themselves of the rags of time!
Even to detachment the heart can be attached, God knows,
For the heart is a net spread for misery.
Transform my heart to a placeless place of safety,
Carry it to the mountains where it dies into You.
Come quickly! My body's tired of this country;
Make it drunk, set it free, call to it, "Come quickly!"
Offer me a cup overflowing with the wine of wonder
So I can no longer tell my head from my feet.
Don't give me bread, or water, or peace, or sleep;
Thirst for You is blood-money for a hundred souls like mine.
Today, my Beloved, you have swept me to Your table
Let me stammer and stagger at the Glory of Your Feast.
News has raced through the city: Today's the Day of Joy!
You are an ass if you want anything but God,
A sad and crazy ass trying to get fat on ash;
Know that the grass of ash dirties the mouth that eats it.
Remember, always, what Mohammed said:
"Stay away from the green of filthy places!"
Beloved, I am far from the grass of the ashpits
I am far from the houris of the gardens
I am far from pride, far from vanity;
I am drunk on the wine of the Divine Majesty.

The thought of a final Beauty leaps like a deer in my heart
Like the moon racing up the sky, like a lily
Lifting its head suddenly from the river grass.
See, all the world's images are running to Your Image
Scraps of iron drawn by a magnet of light.
Diamond becomes stone before You, lions small flowers;
The sun before You shrinks tinier than any atom.
In You, this whole world blazes now like Mount Sinai,
Each of its atoms foams over with fire-water
Each soul becomes Moses lost in the Vision of God.
Each creature is soldered to You and its own Origin,
Laughing at Nothingness and clapping its own miracle.
Each leaf opens fresh and bright, each atom sings its discovery:
"Resignation is the key to happiness,
Grace is the door to the peace beyond the mind."

I and Eternal Love

I and Eternal Love were born into the Universe
From one Light-Womb; I may seem a new Lover,
But I am older than the two worlds.

O season of sweet rains, rains fragrant as musk,
Pour down, now, on all the friends of the Beloved!
You are the tears of separation, of passion,
You will water the dry mountain of the heart.
O eye of storm-clouds! Pour your tears like a pitcher!
How you envy our friends with their faces like moons.
See this cloud that weeps! Gaze on this laughing garden!
Our sick are saved by the tears of heaven.
Look how the dark cloud has poured life to all the thirsty,
How a vast cup pours wine for those whose heart is light!
Heaven has spread its pearls over the plains of Misery.
This cloud is like Jacob, this flower like Joseph in the field.
It is our tears of longing that make Joseph's face so radiant
One of these teardrops will become pearl, another narcissus;
The hands of those who take ours will fill warm with gold.
Yesterday, the garden was flooded with fresh splendor
Because the Lovers were abandoned and drunk all day.
Close your lips like a shell, you drunkard! Don't move!
Let all the souls awoken to the Invisible
Cluster round you in sweet fragrant fire!

Beyond the Seven Hundred Veils

The Light of God has seven hundred veils. Think of these veils of Light as so many "degrees." Behind each of these veils, there is a certain category of saint, and their veils are lifted "by degrees" as they progress, rung by rung.

Those on the lowest rung cannot bear the Light in front of them because they have weak eyes. Those on the next rung—because their eyes also are weak—cannot bear any stronger light.

The Light that is life itself for the saint on the highest rung is agony and ordeal for the one with bad eyes. Slowly, however, his sight will improve and become stronger. When he has gone beyond the seven hundred veils, he will become the Sea.

May Our Nights Give Birth

In the invisible world, there are marvelous, strange things, and nights grow pregnant with wonders. These engender searing nostalgia in the heart and visions in the mind, and anyone who comes to know these prays with every breath that that which exists in the invisible world—and with which the nights are heavy—will be born and flare out here and transfigure this world and all its laws and conditions. O Divine Beloved, establish Your Justice everywhere! Break down and remake us all in Your Image of Eternal Love! Make us, O King of Kings, servants of your all-transforming Alchemy!

King of our body and soul
Who opens our lips in laughter
Who rings our eyes with kohl
Whose majesty humiliates the moon,
Whose love has the right to spill our blood,
When I saw You my heart cried out in ecstasy:
"What I wanted and feared most has come true!"
We are balls in the curve of your polo-stick:
Sometimes you swing us to anguish, sometimes to joy;
Sometimes you roll us into the pit of sleep,
Sometimes you swerve us to savage darkening pleasures.
Sometimes you usher us into the City of Eternity,
Sometimes you drive us over the plains of Annihilation.
Sometimes we praise you and sometimes we lament;
Sometimes we are the slave of desire, sometimes drunk on You.
It is You who has created the soul;
It is You who has driven it wild and crazy.
Sometimes the Lover stays secluded in retreat,
Sometimes he flashes out in every form and shape.
Sometimes he aspires to the crown of gold;
Sometimes he pours dust and ashes on his head.
The soul is a strange tree: it can produce apples or gourds;
Sometimes she produces poison, sometimes sugar,
Sometimes agony, sometimes healing.
Sometimes she weaves in the heart the web of Awareness,
Sometimes she tears from it every thread of clarity.
Sometimes she engenders knowledge after knowledge
Sometimes she wipes away all things in negation.
One day she is a saint, the next a leopard or hyena.
Sometimes she is an enemy, more cruel than death,
Sometimes her eyes are softer than a mother's.

Sometimes she's thorn, sometimes rose;
Sometimes vinegar, sometimes clear wine.
Sometimes she beats the drum, sometimes she *is* the drum;
Sometimes she is Jesus, sometimes a charlatan with no teeth.
The home of fish is the sea
The sea is the soul's garden and country.
The sea will be her shroud and tomb;
Everything but sea for her is a torment and ordeal.
She flees all the colors of a dying world
And steeps herself in the dyes of Jesus.
She has turned to God's own color, since God
    "does what He wants."
She has abandoned shame and shamelessness, "near" or "far."
She has escaped "go" and "come" like the still millwheel.
We have opened a door in front of you,
    don't send our friends away;
This door of words creaks with rust: say "Silence is best!"

Of Angels, the One Mind, and the One Secret

Mind and Angel are related. The Angel may have a definite form, light, feathers, wings, while Mind has not—but in reality Mind and Angel are One, one in nature and one in the way they act.

If you could dissolve an Angel, you would dissolve it into Mind—nothing would remain of its feathers and wings. Angels are all Mind, in fact, embodied Mind. They are embodied intelligences.

Think of a bird made of wax. It may be marvelously made, every feather a different accurate miracle, but still it is wax. And when you melt it down, its beak, feathers, wings all revert to being the wax they were made from. Nothing remains that can be named or separated or differentiated; everything becomes wax, original wax.

Ice works in the same way. When you melt it, it becomes water. When it is water you can't grasp it, it slips through your fingers. When it is frozen, you can hold it and store it. But still it remains water, in a different shape.

All things in all worlds are the forms of Mind. When His Face flashes out and all the horizons melt and vanish, then you will know who you are and who He is, and that there is no difference. He who knows himself knows his Lord.

Then, all around you and in all things and events, the One Secret will be ceaselessly revealing itself, in mystery after mystery.

Dive Again and Again

The second you stepped into this world of existence
A ladder was placed before you to help you escape it.
First, you were mineral; then you transformed into a plant;
Then you became an animal. (How could you not know this?)
Then you changed yet again, and became a human being
Endowed with divine consciousness, reason, faith.
Look at your body, made from dust: what perfection it has!
And when you have gone beyond being human
You will, without any doubt, become an Angel;
You will be done with earth, and Heaven will be your home.
Go beyond even that angelic condition
Dive again into God's boundless Ocean
So your drop of water at last transforms into the Sea.

My friends! My friends! However hard you look
You'll not find a trace of human nature in me!
Even the maddest madman could never imagine
What I have imagined in my heart!
I am so extreme, even madmen flee me now!
For I have mingled with death, soared and soared in Non-Being.

You have arrived at the dungeons of the heart; stop here.
You have seen the moon and lived; stop here.
You have dragged your rags everywhere; stop here.
You have heard so much talk, so much; stop here.
Gaze at this beauty now, it is His Vision
That makes you visible or invisible; stop here.
The milk running in your breast
Is the milk you drank in from His; stop here.

"I Am with the Patient"

Don't be sad any longer, your sadness is blasphemy,
Blasphemy against the Hand of Splendor
  pouring you joy. . . .
Why batter your head forever against the jail wall?
Look, the door has swung open to a rose garden
A mystery of Light is melting the barred windows.
Why go on gaping and slavering like a whore
At the fading paintings on the bathhouse wall?
Spit at the moon: the spit flies back in your eyes;
Try to tear His robe, it's your own that tatters.
A million million fools boil angrily in this Cauldron
Don't you know yet resignation is the way to Truth?
One day a hedgehog swallowed the tail of a snake,
Threw back its head, rolled itself into a ball.
And what did the snake do? Poor idiot!
It rammed itself against the hedgehog's spines
And screamed and died, riddled all over with wounds.
Had it had patience, it might have wriggled free.
Be careful! Be calm! Pray! Say this to yourself:
"Even the eye of the hurricane closes in the end."
The Lord of the worlds has promised: "I am with the Patient."
O Patient One, grace us a drop of your Patience.
I've given you all I know; now you must do what you can.
Silence! My Lover is smiling: that smile makes all words ash.

Each Moment, Revelation

Each moment, Revelation flashes from heaven to the soul:
"How long will you live like dregs in wine. Rise up!"
Your sins make you heavy like dregs; burn them in Love!
Rise, clapping your hands, to the top of the jar.
Don't constantly stir up mud, if you want your water clear;
Let your dregs become transparent, let your grief settle.
There is a soul like a flame; its smoke is greater than its light;
When there's too much smoke, there's no more light in the house.
Lessen that smoke, Flame will leap through and bless you.
Don't you know yet? It is Your Light that lights the worlds.
Stare into filthy water, and how can you expect
Ever to see the moon or heaven?
The moon and heaven hide when the air grows dark;
Its the North Wind's breath that scours the air pure,
The morning breeze that sweeps all clouds from dawn.
It is tears of longing that clean the mirror of the heart.
Pray, pray always: Prayer and adoration are your breath.
If your breathing stops a moment, your life will end.
The soul in its exile longs for its kingdom beyond space—
Why does its animal half feed so long in fields of death?
Your essential soul is noble; how long will you look in darkness?
You are the royal eagle: Listen, the King is whistling for you.

Happy Endings Are for Those Who Believe

God's Eternal Grace always, in the end, transforms agony into remedy, grief into healing, and destruction into prosperity. When it comes to His saints and prophets and to those who are turned toward His Face in all matters, and whose confidence in His mysterious goodness never for a moment falters, God tests their resignation by sending them calamity after calamity.

When they are reduced to desperation, their enemies mock them, saying: "How you used to praise the boundless grace of God! Look at you! How afflicted and abandoned you are! What help is your savior bringing you now?"

The real lovers of God reply: "Yes, we are weak and shattered, and because of our earthly soul we are in misery and groan and wail, sometimes, with real despair; yet, in the depths of our soul, we possess—and are possessed by—an inviolable trust, firm and brilliant as diamond, because we remember and believe the promise of God who is Justice Itself. In the end, we know that He will turn this poison into sugar, that He will transform these tormented shadows into the purest spring sunlight, and that He will, with His own careful hands, piece together our shattered destiny."

In the end it is the Lovers, not the cynics, who understand fate; everything they said comes to pass. Happy endings are for those who believe and go on and on believing. The Lovers *were* victorious, the help of God did arrive; in exchange for each grief and humiliation, each mockery and misery, they received a hundred thousand fertile and extravagant tendernesses. In return for each separation they found a thousand unions. In the dung of Ruin flowered the Rose of Fruition.

And When I Traveled

Suddenly, in the sky at dawn, a moon appeared,
Descended from the sky
Turned its burning gaze on me,
Like a hawk during the hunt seizing a bird,
Grabbed me and flew with me high into heaven.
When I looked at myself, I could not see myself
For in this moon, my body, by grace, had become soul.
And when I traveled in this soul, I saw nothing but moon
Until the mystery of eternal theophany lay open to me.
All the nine heavenly spheres were drowned in this moon;
The skiff of my being drowned, dissolved, entirely, in that Sea.
Then that Sea broke up into waves, Intelligence danced back
And launched its song.
And the Sea covered over with foam,
And from each bubble of foam something sprang, clothed in form.
Something sprang from each light-bubble, clothed in a body.
Then each bubble of body-foam received a sign from the Sea,
Melted immediately and followed the flow of its waves.
Without the saving, redeeming help of my Lord,
Shams-ul-Haqq of Tabriz,
No one can contemplate the moon, no one can become the Sea.

The World of Origin

Some people are glad when the rose breaks into bloom and fans awake its secret splendor; some are glad when its petals fall back and rejoin Origin.

Some people are happy when friendship, passion, belief, and unbelief no longer exist, for then they can marry Origin and live in its peace. Even the values we love and celebrate most fervently can become walls between us and Him, darkened fountains of narrowness, of duality.

The world of Origin is an always-flowing river of Breadth and Unity. Long ago, tired of discriminations, I chose Unity as my house and Breadth as the water for my ablutions.

Long ago, exhausted by duality, I buried my head in the Sun.

Long ago, worn to a husk by likes and dislikes, I died into the Love that cannot die and that casts no shadow.

The Universal Soul met a separate soul
And placed a pearl on her breast.
And through this touch the soul, like Mary,
Became pregnant with a heart-ravishing Messiah.

The Lord of the Palace will not grant me an audience
The confidant of the soul will not whisper me His secrets.
His charm, His goodness, His glory, His fiery eyes,
And the tender subtlety of His tyranny have all enslaved me.
He mocked me: "Where is *your* love, *your* radiance, *your* glory?"
How can any of my glory remain when I see nothing but Him?
I have drowned in His Sea of Lavishness, I am the slave of His Dawn.
He is the wild perfumed rose who drew me to the rose garden.
Drowning in His Sea, all clothes are heavier than iron—
How heavy my turban is to me now, and my robe!
The Kingdom and its treasures, visionary beauties with soft faces,
All are mine, are mine, when my Friend is in me.
Keep your feasts and your ranks, your brilliances and your talk,
Keep your lion and your burning bush;
I want only my gazelle of Tartary.
He has destroyed me, given me life, stripped me of heart and hands;
He pours me wine, makes me drunk.
He is the assassin who breaks my bones;
He is the cupbearer whose wine heals all agony.
O treacherous heart! Don't do evil and reproach Him!
Don't make me known in the marketplace, don't tell my secrets.
For if you do, He will shatter these fragile chains
And forge fresh ones more terrible and strange.
Don't talk of "duality," don't speak of "two"—
We are one mouth, He and I, one prayer, one glance,
One dancing fiery mountain of fragrance.

Flee greed and desire; both "life" and "death" are plagues.
Dead or alive, my only country is God's Grace.
I have slipped the jeweled noose of these songs
Thrown them and their meanings into the Great Sea.
What are they but rind for a thick bark of scales?
Authentic thought leaps behind and sings in secret!
O silence! You are what is most precious in me!
You are the veil of all my real wealth!
Why parade knowledge? Be silent, for in silence
There is neither fear nor hope nor gain nor loss.
Does a king tithe a destroyed and abandoned village?
I am abandoned and destroyed, more than any words can describe;
Don't scavenge in my words for any value or wisdom.
Without destroying me, how could He pour me this treasure?
He had to throw me to the waves for Love's Sea to sweep me away.
What can the man of words guess of the sweetness of silence?
What can the arid heart know of always-flowing freshness?
I am the mirror, I am the mirror, I am not a man of words—
You'll know my spiritual state when your ears become gaze.
I wave my hands like leaves, I whirl dancing like the moon;
My turning may seem earthly, but it is purer, far purer,
Than the turning of all the spheres of heaven.
You go on talking if you want; I'll pray to God for your soul,
When wild and drunk I bow down to Him each morning.
I will give you my shirt, I swear, and my robe;
Whatever the King graces me, I will share with you.
From the King's hand comes to me directly
The cup and jar of Eternal Wine—
The source of the sun itself begs me for a mouthful.
I am silent, my throat is sick, you go on talking if you have to.
You are the voice of David, I'm just a jet of scattering straw.

The Conscious Bow

There are some people who are vain enough to believe that a person creates his or her own acts, and that every act they perform is their own creation.

This is nonsense. Whatever we do, we do through an instrument—our reason, our body, or our spirit. Did we assemble and create these? Of course not! Can we act without these? Of course not!

The creator of our acts is not us, but God. You may think that everything you do, good or evil, you have chosen to do, and in a certain sense you have. About the consequences of any of your good or evil actions, however, you have absolutely no idea. For example, you may pray to be safe in the next world and secure in this—but the benefit of your prayer will not be limited to the things you ask for; your prayer will radiate a hundred thousand graces which you cannot know. Only God can know what these graces are, and it is God who prompted you to pray in the first place.

A human being is like a bow in the hands of omnipotence. God uses him or her for different tasks; the real agent is always God, not the bow. The bow is ignorant and unconscious of God, so the order of the world can be kept going.

The greatest bow is the one who is conscious of Whose Hand it is in.

Always Keep in Awe

One day the Prophet questioned the Angel Gabriel about his inner state. Gabriel replied, "At this moment, I find myself in such a state of fear and reverence before the Divine Grandeur that I feel like a bedraggled sparrow."

Mohammed was astonished and said to Gabriel: "But you are an angel and angels are immaterial pure light; you are not a slave of your carnal soul and do not stagger under the burden of a dying body! How can you experience fear?"

Gabriel replied: "The grandeur of God is so immense that it captured the Angel Azrael and made the Angels Harut and Marut tumble from the height of Heaven into the pit of Babylon."

O Bird, whose call raises the dead,
Nightingale with your voice of night and musk—
Ravish Venus with that song
Whose every note is new life!
Show Your Beauty, Moon of God,
So friends and enemies can witness it
With whitened faces and eyes dark with tears.
Grief and longing make all men groan:
"Save us from the agony this tyrant inflicts
Beautiful and terrible as a dragon!"
You have made grief's lute sing out
With the sharp and heavy sounds of your "Go away!"
Nothingness, through You, births these songs of pure passion,
Time's darkness is adorned with their luminous tears.
Cupbearer! Never forget us! Fill the worlds with your breath!
Archangel of the Heart, make clay and water live!
Breathe into our ears the divine breath of Love!
We are tumbled haystacks, Lord, corn confused with straw;
Blow on us, separate us,
Send grief to grief, and joy to joy
So mind sinks back to mind, and the heart soars to heaven.

O sudden Resurrection! O boundless, endless, compassion!
You, who set the Bush of the Mind on fire
Have come at last, key to this vast prison.
You blaze among the poverty-stricken like gold,
Chamberlain of the Sun, heart of all hope.
You are the sought and the seeker, the beginning, the end;
You have erupted softly in the heart of the heart,
Threaded all thought on your diamond laughter.
O incomparable Giver of Life, cut Reason loose at last!
Let it wander grey-eyed from vanity to vanity.
Shatter open my skull, pour in it the wine of madness!
Let me be mad, as mad as You, mad with You, with us.
Beyond the sanity of fools is a burning desert
Where Your Sun is whirling in every atom; drag me there,
Beloved, drag me there, let me roast in Perfection!

When Your image dances into my heart
How many drunken images seethe along with it!
They whirl around Your image, Your moon-like splendor
     whirling at the center.
When an image brushes against You, it returns the sun's rays
     like a mirror.
My words become drunk through one of Your qualities,
Stagger a thousand times between tongue and heart, heart
     and tongue.
My words are drunk, my heart is drunk, and Your images
     are drunk—
They all pile up on top of each other, and just gaze.

Your Soul Is So Close to Mine

Your soul is so close to mine
I know what you dream.
Friends scan each other's depths;
Would I be a Friend, if I didn't?
A Friend is a mirror of clear water;
I see my gains in you, and my losses.
Turn away from me for one moment
My mouth fills and chokes with gall.
Like a dream that flows from heart to heart,
I, too, flow continually through all hearts.
Everything you think, I know;
Your heart is so close to mine.
I have other symbols, even more intimate,
Come closer still, dare to invoke them.
Come, like a real dervish, and dance among us,
Don't joke, don't boast I am already present.
In the center of your house I am like a pillar,
On your rooftop I bow my head like a gutter.
I turn like a cup in the heart of your assembly;
In the thick of your battles, I strike like an arrow.
When I give my life for yours, what Grace descends!
Each life I give gives you a thousand new worlds!
In this house, there are thousands of corpses
You sit and say: "Here is my kingdom."
A handful of dust moans "I was hair."
Another handful whispers: "I was bones."
Another cries: "I was old."
Yet another: "I was young."
Another shouts: "Stop where you are! Stop!
Don't you know who I am! I am so-and so's son!"
You sit destroyed, astounded, and then suddenly Love appears.
"Come closer still," Love says, "it is I, Eternal Life."

This Is Your Own Voice

Define and narrow me, you starve yourself of yourself.
Nail me down in a box of cold words,
    that box is your coffin.
I do not know who I am.
I am in astounded lucid confusion.
I am not a Christian, I am not a Jew, I am not a Zoroastrian,
And I am not even a Muslim.
I do not belong to the land, or to any known or unknown sea.
Nature cannot own or claim me, nor can heaven;
Nor can India, China, Bulgaria.
My birthplace is placelessness,
My sign to have and give no sign.
You say you see my mouth, ears, eyes, nose—they are not mine.
I am the life of life.
I am that cat, this stone, no one.
I have thrown duality away like an old dishrag,
I see and know all times and worlds
As one, one, always one.
So what do I have to do to get you to admit who is speaking?
Admit it and change everything!
This is your own voice echoing off the walls of God.

My Hidden Face

It is said that a certain S., a professor, used to stand stock-still gazing astonishedly at Rumi, while the other Friends went on with the ritual dance. One day Rumi asked him: "Why do you gaze at my face with such intensity and not dance?" The professor bowed low to him and shyly replied, "There is no other face in the whole universe but your holy face that I could think of looking at or contemplating. Nowhere else can I find the joy that finds and opens me when I gaze at you."

Rumi smiled. "I have another face, a secret and hidden face, which cannot be seen by earthly eyes. Direct all your efforts steering your being towards that Face and to perceiving it, until the moment when my visible face disappears; then, you will be able to see clearly that hidden Face, and when you see it, you will recognize me."

The Story of the Argument between the Byzantines and the Chinese in the Art of Painting and Making Portraits

The Chinese boasted: "We're the greater artists." The Byzantines claimed: "Ours is the true power and the real perfection."

"I will put you both to the test," said the Sultan. "That will show clearly whose claim is just."

At first the Chinese and Byzantines argued noisily, but the Byzantines fell silent.

Then the Chinese said: "Let us have one full room for us, and another room for our rivals. Then we'll see who's best."

There were two rooms, whose doors faced each other; the Chinese took one, the Byzantines the other.

The Chinese begged the King to give them a hundred colors; the King opened his treasure-chests and let them take what they wanted.

Every morning, through his lavishness, what the Chinese needed was supplied them from his treasury.

The Byzantines declared: "We don't need color and we don't need paint; all we need to do is to remove all dirt."

So they shut their door and started to polish the walls until they became pure and brilliant like a cloudless spring sky.

There is a path from the mixing to the absence of colors; color is like clouds, its absence like the moon.

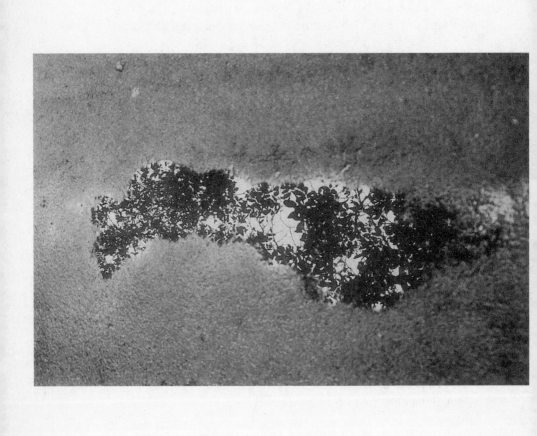

Whatever light and splendor you glimpse in clouds, know it comes from the stars and sun and moon.

When the Chinese had completed their work, they were ecstatic and started to sing and beat drums.

The King came in and saw what they had painted, and the vision made him drunk with joy.

Then, he went to where the Byzantines were; the curtain separating the two rooms was drawn back.

On those walls pure of any stain appeared the reflection of the Chinese paintings.

Everything that had astounded the Sultan in the other room seemed even more magnificent here; he wept with wonder.

The Byzantines are the Sufis: they aren't erudite, don't study or read, but they have polished their hearts and washed them pure of desire, greed, avarice, and hate.

What is this purity of the mirror? The Heart that receives innumerable images.

This Moses keeps in his breast the infinite, formless form of the invisible reflected in the mirror of his Heart.

Although this form cannot be contained in heaven, or in the heaven beyond heaven, or in the starry spheres, or in the globe that rests on the fish—

All these worlds and dimensions are numbered and limited; the mirror of the Heart is limitless.

Here, all understanding falls silent if it doesn't want to betray; for the Heart is with God, or rather, the Heart *is* God.

The reflection of each image shines eternally out of the heart alone, as much in the many as in the One beyond it.

Polish your heart and you'll soar above all color and perfume; you will contemplate Beauty ceaselessly; you will abandon the form and rind of consciousness, and unfurl the flag of Certainty.

When the forms of the Eight Paradises flame out, you will know your heart's tablets are receptive.

From heaven, the starry spheres, the void, you will receive, continually, hundreds of impressions. Why do I say impressions? I mean: the direct vision of God.

One day, Rumi asked a young disciple to bring him a tray of delicacies. He took it, covered it with a cloth and walked away. "I followed him at a distance," the young disciple tells us, "and he went into some ruins where a dog had given birth. There I was amazed by his compassion and pity. 'For seven days,' he told me, 'this miserable creature has not eaten, and because of her children she can't go off and look for food. It is God who brought her cries to my ears and ordered me to console her.'"

One day, in the middle of a large crowd in the market of Konya, Rumi was teaching mystical truths. At the time of the evening prayer, as night fell, a group of dogs formed a circle around him. As he gazed at them and went on with his explanations, they wagged their tails and shook their heads and groaned with delight. Rumi said: "I swear by God, the Most High, the All-Powerful, that these dogs understand my inmost meaning!" He added, "These doors and these walls proclaim the praise of God and understand His divine secrets! Door and wall say subtle things; fire, water, and earth tell sublime stories!"

The Water, the Door, and the Shield

Call that man absorbed when the water has total control of him and he has no control whatsoever of the water. A swimmer and an absorbed being are both in the water; but while the swimmer uses his own strength and moves where he wants, the absorbed person is carried along, directed, and buoyed up by the water alone.

Every movement and action of the absorbed person springs not from him but from the water; he is present only as a screen for its working. If you were to hear words coming out of a wall, you would know that they do not come out of the wall itself but that there is someone who is making the wall seem to speak.

God's saints have died before dying and become like a door or a wall. Not a hair of separate existence remains in them.

In the hands of the All-Powerful they are wielded like shields; when a shield moves, it is the hand that moves it. Revere someone who is a shield of this kind as a part of God; never be violent against God. Those who batter such a shield have declared war on God and deployed their powers against Him. They will end badly, like Pharaoh, for the shield is designed to stand firm until the Resurrection.

The Briefcase of the Real Saint

A king said to a dervish, "When total revelation is graced you, and you come into the nearness of God, remember me." The dervish answered: "When I step into that Presence and the Light of the Sun of that Splendor shines on me, I will no more even remember myself. How do you expect me to remember you?"

Yet it is true that when God has chosen a servant and made him absorbed in Him, if anyone tugs his sleeve and asks the servant something, even if that saint does not explicitly talk of him to God, his petition will be granted.

A king had a servant he trusted and loved. Whenever this servant set out for the palace, people would crowd around him and hand him letters explaining their miseries and requests. He would stuff all of these into a briefcase. When this servant actually came into the presence of the king, he was so overwhelmed by the glory of his beauty that he would faint. The king would then, very lovingly, put his hand into his servant's briefcase and say: "What has he here, this faithful and astounded servant of mine, this lover who is overwhelmed by my beauty?" So, in this way, the king would find the letters and endorse everyone's petitions, and then put back the letters in the briefcase; and, in this way, no request made to the servant was ever rejected; in fact the petitioners demands were satisfied lavishly, and they received much more than they had ever thought of asking for.

In the case of other servants, however, who remained conscious in the king's presence and could explain to him the stories and needs of the people, out of a hundred affairs and petitions perhaps only one would be fulfilled.

Flowers from Another Country

Rumi's wife, Kira Khatoun, used to tell this story:

"During one winter, our Master went into retreat with Shams. He was leaning on Shams' knees, talking; I was listening to them through a crack in the door, trying to understand what they were saying. All at once I saw the wall of the house open and six astonishing Beings came in to greet my husband and Shams, and placed before the Master a bouquet of marvelous flowers. They stayed seated until the midday prayers without saying a word. After prayers, the Beings stood up, bowed with respect, and left by the way they came—through the wall. I fainted with terror. When I returned to myself, I saw the Master standing in front of me, handing out to me the bouquet and saying, 'Keep it.'

"Immediately, I sent a sample of the bouquet to the druggist, with a note that I had never seen such flowers and wanted to know what they were and where they came from. At the shop, everyone was astonished by their color, freshness, and fragrance, and wondered how on earth they could flourish in mid-winter. In the shop there was a well-known merchant, Cheref-ed-din Hindi, who was always going to India on business and bringing back from there rare and wonderful things. When he was shown the flowers he cried, 'Why, they are from India! They are grown in an area near Ceylon. How did they find their way to Asia Minor?' My servant took back the flowers and reported their replies; my astonishment grew. Then, suddenly, our Master came in and said: 'Keep this bouquet tightly bound together and never show it to any profane eyes, for the people who brought it for you are Hidden Ones of the Sanctuary of Generosity, the Master of India, and they have brought them especially for you, to serve as food for the palace of your soul, and to give strength to your eyes and body.'"

It is said that Kira Khatoun kept the flowers until her death. Some of them, however, she gave—with the Master's permission—

to Gurdhi-Khatoun, the Sultan's wife. Whenever anyone suffered from eye sickness, she would rub the infected part with a petal, and it healed immediately.

The color and fragrance of the flowers never diminished.

The Tent, the Slavegirl, and the Really Awake

The words of the great saints differ in a thousand ways in their form, but as God is One and the Way is One, there cannot be two different sets of words. In their form, they may appear opposed, but in their meaning they are one. All sense of "difference" derives from the form; in the essential meaning, there is only and always harmony.

A prince wanted a tent made. One person twists the rope, another hammers the pegs in, yet another weaves the material for the tent. Everyone seems to be doing something completely different, yet in fact they are all engaged in the same task. This is what the doings of this world are like. When you really look into it, you will see that everyone is doing God's will, whether they are saints or devils, debauchees or holy-hearted. Think of a king who has to test the fidelity and trustworthiness of his subjects: doesn't he need a tempter? If his subjects were never tempted, he would never know if they really were loyal or not. So, you see, the tempter is really doing the will of the king. The king sends a storm to see who is stable and who is shifty; to separate, in other words, the mosquito from the tree and the rose garden, so the mosquito can disappear and only the hawk remain.

Another example: a king once ordered a slavegirl to cover herself with silks and jewels and offer herself to his slaves, so he could find out which of them were loyal. What the girl did appears outwardly sinful, but in fact she is serving the king's purpose.

As the Koran says: "There is nothing that does not proclaim His praise." True servants of God know this, and know truth face-to-face and without any veil. They know that all human beings, both good and evil, are obedient slaves of God. For them, this world is already the Resurrection. Resurrection means serving God and never doing anything that is not His service. The Holy and Awake see this truth even here, in this world of masks and illusions; for them, even if all veils were removed between them and the Real, their faith would not in any way be increased.

The Veiled Ones

☀ People keep telling me, "We saw Shams of Tabriz, we really did see him." Idiots! How on earth do they imagine they could have seen him? And where? A person who could not see a camel on the roof of a house swaggers in and claims, "I saw the hole of a needle and then threaded it." Do you know the story about the man who said, "Two things make me laugh—a black man painting his nails black, and a blind man putting his head out the window"? Well, these people are like that man. Inwardly blind, they gaily put their heads out the window of their bodies. Who could they see? Who cares about their approval or disapproval?

The first necessary thing is to acquire real sight. How can you do this except through devotion, surrender, and hard work? Then you have to look. And even when you *do* look you may not be able to see. Not everything is meant to be visible. There are many advanced saints in this world, who live in union with God; and then there are those even further on who are named the Veiled Ones of God. Those who live in union are always praying: "Please, God, show me one of your Veiled Ones!" As long as their whole being is not one fire of longing, or as long as God intends, however hard they look they will not be able to see anything. As for those other whores of gnosis who claim effortlessly to see, know, and understand everything—how can we begin to take them seriously? The most holy are nearly always hidden, hidden in a cloud of humility and Divine Protection. How can anyone see any one of them without their or God's will?

Trust very few people who talk about saints and God. The marketplace is crawling with false fakirs and dervishes half-crazed with vanity. No wonder God has hidden the Veiled Ones! Would you expose your most fragile and beautiful treasures to the eyes of vulgarians?

No "Above" or "Below"

The really holy never need to be honored; their selves are already honored by Love. If a lamp wants to be placed where it can be seen, it wants that for others' sake, not its own. What does the lamp care whether it is placed "above" or "below"? Wherever it is, it is still a lamp and it still gives out light. Nevertheless, it wants its light to reach and help others. Imagine if the sun were below the earth—it would still be the sun, of course, but the world would languish in darkness. So the sun is placed in its regal position not for its own sake at all, but for the world's. The real holy ones who are put in high positions are like the lamp and the sun—they do not care about "high" or "low," "above" or "below," and do not look to be revered by others.

Whenever Vision unfurls its ecstatic flag in you, or your mind blazes from a lightning flash of grace from heaven, you are, in that moment, cold to "above" and "below," to all status and rank, mastery or leadership, all man-made titles, praises, elevations, honors. None of these things concern you: you soar like a hawk in the cloudless sky of union.

If such splendor breaks over ordinary seekers, imagine how little the really holy ones, who are the mines themselves of that Love and that Splendor, could possibly care for "below" and "above"! No categories of any kind chain or even interest them; all their glorying is in God, and God is utterly free of anything we know as "above" or "below." "Above" and "below" belong to those of us who have heads and feet and deluded imaginations in the service of the tyrants of our false selves. Mohammed, may he always rest in peace, said once: "Do not make me out to be greater than Jonah, just because his ascension was in a whale's belly while mine took place in Heaven and on the Throne." What the Prophet meant was this: "For God, the whale's belly is the same as the Throne."

God's Words

When Mansur Al-Hallaj's love of God had become perfect, he became his own enemy and annihilated himself. He said: "I am the Supreme Reality"—that is, "I have vanished, God alone remains." This is not pride, as some fools have thought it, nor madness, as even bigger fools have pretended—it is the most extreme humility and represents the final limit of servanthood, for it means: "Only He is."

Real arrogance consists in saying: "You are God and I am your Servant." Saying this, you cannot help but affirm your own existence, and dualism follows necessarily upon that. If you say "He is God," that too leads to dualism; until "I" exists, "He" is impossible. So it was God who said: "I am God." Anything or anyone other than God was not alive in Mansur; "Mansur" had vanished. Those words were God's words.

On the Endless Path in God
Don't stay in any of the stations,
Don't stay in any station you have won—
Go on! Go on! Desire more and more!
The man who has dropsy can never have enough water.
The Divine Courtyard is the infinite plane;
Leave behind you the place of honor.
What is the real place of honor? The Path itself.

No End

The goal of travelers is to reach their destination; what could be the destination or end to those who have attained Union, in which there can never be any separation?

They travel on and on, from bliss to finer bliss, from knowledge to ignorance to wilder knowledge, from peace to ever-deepening and expanding peace.

A vain fool came to me and said: "I have attained Union! My journey is over!" I said: "Never blaspheme like that again! If you had attained union, your real journey would just be beginning!" But why throw pearls on a dung-heap?

The journey to Him ends with the revelation of His Glory; the journey *in* Glory can never ever end, for Glory is boundless and its wonders are infinite.

And the Law is: No ripe grape ever again becomes unripe; no mature fruit ever again becomes green.

The Three States

Human beings have three spiritual states. In the first, a person pays no attention whatsoever to God and worships anything—sex, money, rank—*but* God. When he starts to learn something deeper, then he will serve no one and nothing but God. And when he progresses in this state he grows silent; he doesn't claim: "I don't serve God," nor does he boast "I do serve God"; he has gone beyond these two positions. From such beings, no sound comes into this world.

The Stations of Security

A pilgrim who reaches the Kaaba is better than the one who is still wandering in the desert. The latter is still afraid, uncertain whether he will reach his goal or not; the former has attained what he set out for, he has reached the Kaaba. One certainty is better than a thousand doubts.

He who has not yet arrived still has hope, but how can you compare a merely hopeful man to one who has arrived? There is an abyss between fear and security. This is obvious; what may not be obvious is that there are also subtle gradations between different stations of security. The station that Mohammed was graced is higher and more exalted than any of the other prophets, although all of them can be said to be in security and to have gone beyond fear. The Koran says: "We have elevated some above others."

It is possible to make a map of the different states and stations of fear and show, more or less accurately, how through grace, devotion, and progressive revelation, fear slowly transforms into security; the stations of security, however, are signless. In our world of fear, everyone decides exactly what he or she is going to spend on the Path of God. One decides to spend his wealth, another her health, another his life; another man will fast, or pray, or do ritual prostrations. The rewards of each of these decisions can be indicated, as their stages are distinct in form. In the same way, the stages between Konya and Caesarea are separate, distinct, and well-known; first you go to Qaimaz, then to Uprukh, then to Sultan, and so on. But the stages by sea from Antalya to Alexandria are without any sign. The captain of the ship knows them, of course, but he cannot tell them to people who come from the land, for they would not understand.

Attain the Musk through Its Fragrance and Become One with It

The Divine Essence is like musk; this material world and its joys are its fragrance. That person is good who has searched for the musk itself and not been satisfied with its fragrance. That person is evil who has contented himself with just owning the fragrance; he has grasped after things which will not remain. What is the fragrance but an attribute of the musk? As long as the musk appears here in the world, then its fragrance intoxicates. When, however, it slips behind the Veil and goes back to the world of Origin, all those who have lived by it perish. The fragrance, after all, is one with the musk and follows after the musk when it disappears.

Blessed is the person who has attained the musk through its fragrance and become one with it. For him there is no earth; he has become eternal in the essence of the musk, and takes on the character and properties of musk. One with it, he spreads its fragrance everywhere, and everyone is restored to true life.

All that survives of this person is his name. Imagine a horse thrown into a salt pit: all that remains of the horse after a while will be an outline; the rest will be turned to salt. The horse's power will then be from the sea of salt with which it is one. If it still has an outline or name, these will not harm it or diminish its salty tang in any way. If you call the salt pit by some other name, it won't lose its salt-hood either.

Action Is a Meaning within a Person

Once the Emir Parvana said to me: "The essence of the whole matter is action." I said to him: "Of course, but where are the people of action? Where are those who are really looking with their entire being for action? Where are they? I want to show them what action is. At the moment, you are looking for words. If I do not provide words and more words, you will get angry. Become a seeker of action! I want to show you action! I am looking all over the world for someone to whom I can really show action. Since no one wants to 'buy' action—only words—I am condemned to traffic in words. What can anyone know of real action who is not a person of real action? Action cannot be known through words, but only through action, just as science can only be known through science, form through form, and meaning through meaning. I do not see anyone taking this road; so how will anyone see if I am on it and in action?"

Action is not prayer and fasting. Prayer and fasting are "forms" of action. What is action? An inner meaning. From Adam's to Mohammed's time, prayer and fasting were not in the form we now know them, but action always was. What is the form of action? Action is a meaning within a person. And when that meaning is one with Love, the Fire of Passion radiates all around and in every dimension, and miracles abound.

Constant Help, Constant Service

The finest human beings are those who constantly help others. The only Master is the one who is the servant of his people.

In the Koran it is written: "Never oppress the orphan. Never push away the beggar." To be just for one hour is worth more than praying for sixty years. And what is justice? Putting each thing in its real place.

Last Words

During his last illness, a friend came to wish Rumi a quick recovery. Rumi replied: "When only this hair-shirt remains between Lover and Beloved, don't you want the Light to unite with the Light?"

And he went on to speak these verses:

> *Why should I be desperate?*
> *Each atom of my being*
> *Has opened in ecstasy!*
> *Why should I be desperate?*
> *Why should I not leave this well?*
> *Don't I have a strong rope?*
> *I have built a birdhouse for the birds of souls.*
> *O bird of my soul! Fly away now!*
> *I possess a hundred fortified towers.*

On Your Feet

On your feet, my friends! Let us go!
It is time to leave this world.
A drum is beating from heaven, calling us, calling us.
Look: the camel-driver's awake, preparing the caravan—
He's hungry to set out. Travelers, why go on sleeping?
All round us swells the ringing of bells, the tumult of farewell;
Each moment, a spirit takes wing to the Place beyond place.
And from those stellar lights, those vast blue vaults of heaven,
Mysterious figures appear to reveal all secret things.

Look at me! I am your companion in the tomb.
On that night you leave your shop and your house,
You will hear my salutation in the tomb,
And you will know then that never
Were you hidden from my eyes.
I am the spark of intelligence and reason in your breast
At the moment of pleasure, at the moment of joy,
At the moment of suffering, at the moment of misery.
And on that strange night when you hear the voice of the Beloved,
You will soar free of the bite of serpents or the terror of ants.
The drunkenness of love will carry into your tomb these gifts:
Wine, the Beloved, a candle, meat and delicacies, and incense.
In that instant the lamp of true knowing is lit
What a tumult rises from the dead in the tombs!
The earth of the cemetery is split open by their cries,
By the beating of the drum of resurrection,
By the glory of the rising of the dead.
They have torn their shrouds to stop their ears from fear.
What is the head, the ear, before the shriek of that trumpet?
Be attentive to where you look, and don't let error in
So that the one who sees and the one who is seen can become One.
Wherever you cast your gaze, you will see my face,
Whether you contemplate yourself or gaze at this tumult,
     give up all deformed vision;
Purify your eyes, for the evil eye will then be far from my beauty.
Take care not to mistake my human form,
For the spirit is subtle and love is jealous.
What is form? Even with a hundred thicknesses of fur,
The rays of the mirror of the soul make the world manifest.
If men had looked for God instead of gold and food,
You would not see one single blind man beside the ditch.

Since you have opened a shop in our town
And are showering us with carnations, do not talk;
Shoot out to all of us your Lover's glances.
I keep silent and hide the secret from the unworthy.
Only you are worthy, for me the mystery is hidden.
Come, come, to the east, like the Sun of Tabriz.
Gaze at the splendors of victory and the standard of triumph.

How Could the Lover Ever Die

I have died, time and time again,
and Your breath has always revived me.
If I die in You a thousand times more,
I will die in the same way.
I was scattered like dust, and then You gathered me;
And how can I die scattered before Your gatheredness?
Like the child that dies at its mother's breast,
I will die at the breast
Of the mercy and the bounty of the All-Merciful.
What am I saying? How could the Lover ever die?

When Lovers die in their journey,
The spirit's king runs out to meet them.
When they die at the feet of that moon,
They all light up like the Sun.

Our death is our wedding with eternity.
What is its secret? God is One.
The sun divides itself
Streaming through the different openings of the house;
But when these openings are closed, multiplicity vanishes.
Multiplicity exists in the separate grapes
But cannot be found in the juice that springs from the grape.
For he who is alive in the Light of God,
The death of this carnal soul is grace.
About this don't say anything either good or bad,
Because this has transcended good and bad.
Fix your gaze on God, only and always,
And do not speak of what is invisible
So that into your gaze He can put another gaze.
It's only the vision of physical eyes
That construct that vision for which nothing invisible
      or secret exists.
Turn your gaze toward the Light of God,
For under such a searchlight, what thing could remain hidden?
Even though all lights emanate from the Divine Light,
Do not call these lights the Light of God.
It is the Eternal Light that is the Light of God;
The ephemeral light is only the attribute of the body and the flesh.
It is the infernal light that glitters in the eyes of creatures
Except of those whom
God himself has anointed their eyes with kohl.
For His friend Abraham, His fire became Light,
The eyes of intelligence are ignorant as the donkey's.
Oh Lord God, who graces the gift of vision,
The bird of vision is flying toward you
On the wings of astounded desire.

Song of Victory

When on the day of my death you carry my bier
Do not imagine my heart has remained in this world.
Do not weep over me, do not say: "Oh, how sad, how sad!"
That would be tumbling into the trap of the devil,
    and that would be sad.
When you see my corpse laid out, don't cry out: "He has gone!"
For union and meeting will then be mine forever.
And as you lower me into my tomb, do not say: "Farewell."
For the tomb veils from us the union of paradise.
My decline you have seen, now discover my soaring ascent!
Would setting cause any harm to the sun or moon?
To you, my death seems a setting, but really it is dawn.
Does the tomb seem a prison to you? It is the liberation of the soul.
Has any seed been sown in the earth that has not one day flowered?
Why doubt? Man also is a buried seed.
What bucket would go down empty without being filled?
The spirit is like Joseph, would he complain of the well?
Keep your mouth closed over here, to open it over there
So that beyond space may thrill your song of victory.

Love's Apocalypse, Love's Glory

One breath from the breath of the Lover
would be enough to burn away the world,
To scatter this insignificant universe like grains of sand.
The whole of the cosmos would become a Sea,
And sacred terror rubble this Sea to nothing.
No human being would remain, and no creature;
A smoke would come from heaven; there would be
    no more man or angel.
Out of this smoke, flame would suddenly flash out
    across heaven.
That second, the sky would split apart and neither space
    nor existence remain.
Vast groans would rise up out of the breast of the universe,
    groans mingled with desolate moaning;
And fire eat up water, and water eat up fire.
The waves of the Sea of the Void would drown in their flood
    the horseman of day and night;
The sun itself fades, vanishes, before this flaming out
    of the soul of man.
Do not ask anyone who is not intimate with the secrets
When the Intimate of the Secret Himself cannot answer you.
Mars will lose its swagger, Jupiter burn the book of the world;
The moon will not hold its empire, its joy will be smirched
    with agony.
Mercury will shipwreck in mud, Saturn burn itself to death;
Venus, singer of heaven, play no longer her songs of joy.
The rainbow will flee, and the cup, and the wine;
There will be no more happiness or rapture,
    no more wound or cure.
Water will no longer dance with light,
    wind no longer sweep the ground;

Gardens no longer abandon themselves to laughter,
    April's clouds no longer scatter their dew.
There will be no more grief, no more consolation,
    no more "enemy" or "witness."
No more flute or song, or lute or mode,
    no more high or low pitch.
Causes will faint away; the cupbearer will serve himself.
The soul will recite: "O my Lord most high!"
The heart will cry out: "My Lord knows best."
Rise up! The Painter of Eternity has set to work one more time
To trace miraculous figures on the crazy curtain of the world.
God has lit a fire to burn the heart of the universe,
The Sun of God has the East for a heart; the splendor of that East
Irradiates at all moments the son of Adam: Jesus, son of Mary.

Just one page remains of the Book of our life
A Word is written in this Book,
A Word radiant with tender Love.
The beauty of this Word astounds even the moon,
Eternal Life glitters on the leaves of the Garden.

Glorious is the moment we sit in the palace, You and I.
Two forms, two faces, but a single soul: You and I.
The flowers will blaze and bird cries shower us
    with immortality
The moment we enter the garden, You and I.
All the stars of heaven will run out to gaze at us
As we burn like the full moon itself, You and I.
The fire-winged birds of heaven will rage with envy
In that place where we laugh ecstatically, You and I.
What a miracle, You and I, entwined in the same nest;
What a miracle, You and I: one Love, one Lover, one Fire,
In this world and the next, in an ecstasy without end.

Helpful Reading

A. J. Arberry. *Discourses of Rumi.* London: John Murray, 1961.
———. *Mystical Poems of Rumi.* First Selection, Poems 1–200. Chicago: University of Chicago Press, 1968.
———. *Mystical Poems of Rumi.* Second Selection, Boulder, Colorado: Westview Press, 1979.

Coleman Barks. *The Essential Rumi.* San Francisco: HarperSanFrancisco, 1995.

W. C. Chittick. *The Sufi Path of Love: The Spiritual Teachings of Rumi.* Albany, N.Y.: State University of New York Press, 1983.

Andrew Harvey. *Love's Fire: Re-Creations of Rumi.* Ithaca, N.Y.: Meeramma, 1988.
———. *Speaking Flame.* Ithaca, N.Y.: Meeramma, 1989.
———. *The Way of Passion: A Celebration of Rumi.* Berkeley, Calif.: Frog, 1994.

R. A. Nicholson. *The Mathnawi of Jalaluddin Rumi.* 8 vols. London: Luzac, 1925–1940.
———. *Rumi, Poet and Mystic.* London: Allen and Unwin, 1952.

Annemarie Schimmel. *I Am Wind, You Are Fire: The Life and Work of Rumi.* Boston: Shambhala, 1992.
———. *The Triumphal Sun.* London: East West, 1978.

Jonathan Star and Shahram Shiva. *A Garden Beyond Paradise: The Mystical Poetry of Rumi.* New York: Bantam Books, 1992.

E. H. Whinfield *The Masnavi, Abridged.* London: Octagon Press, 1973.

Acknowledgments

My deepest thanks to:

Marianne Dresser, dear friend and matchless editor, for her clarity of heart and mind.

Paula Morrison, for her enthusiasm and taste.

Richard Grossinger, for trusting the concept of this book.

Donna Fraser, for all her work.

The California Institute of Integral Studies, for offering me the chance to expand my vision of Rumi.

Karen Kelledjian, for her great open heart and unfailing kindness and loyalty.

Eva de Vitray-Meyerovitch, for many beautiful afternoons in Paris discussing Rumi, and for her wonderful oeuvre.

To all other translators of Rumi—each one of whom has helped me forge my own vision and style, and especially to my friend Coleman Barks for his great work and selfless encouragement.

Kristina Grace, for her friendship and for her championing of my husband Eryk Hanut's photographs.

Leila and Henry Luce, for their love.